Creating Comic Narratives for Stage and Screen

CW00349949

Chris Head

methuen | drama

LONDON · NEW YORK · OXFORD · NEW DELHI · SYDNEY

METHUEN DRAMA
Bloomsbury Publishing Plc
50 Bedford Square, London, WC1B 3DP, UK
1385 Broadway, New York, NY 10018, USA

BLOOMSBURY, METHUEN DRAMA and the Methuen Drama logo are trademarks
of Bloomsbury Publishing Plc

First published in Great Britain 2021

Cover design: Charlotte Daniels
Cover image © iStock

A catalogue record for this book is available from the British Library.

Library of Congress Cataloging-in-Publication Data

Names: Head, Chris, author.
Title: Creating comedy narratives for stage and screen / Chris Head.
Description: London ; New York : Methuen Drama, 2021. | Includes bibliographical references and index. |
Summary: "This accessible and engaging text covering sketch, sitcom and comedy drama, alongside
improvisation and stand-up, brings together a panoply of tools and techniques for creating short and
long-form comedy narratives for live performance, TV and online. Referencing a broad range of comedy
from both sides of the Atlantic, spanning several decades and including material on contemporary
internet sketches, it offers all kinds of useful advice on creating comic narratives for stage and screen:
using life experience as raw material; constructing comedy worlds; creating comic characters, their
relationships and interactions; structuring sketches, scenes and routines; and developing and plotting
stories. The book's interviewees, from the UK and the USA, feature stand-ups, sketch comics,
improvisers and TV comedy producers, and include Steve Kaplan, Hollywood comedy guru and author of
The Hidden Tools of Comedy, Will Hines teacher and improviser from the Upright Citizens Brigade
Theatre and Lucy Lumsden TV producer and former Controller of Comedy Commissioning for BBC.
Written by "the ideal person to nurture new talent" (The Guardian), Creating Comedy Narratives for
Stage & Screen includes material you won't find anywhere else and is a stimulating resource for
comedy students and their teachers, with a range and a depth that will be appreciated by even the most
eclectic and multi-hyphenated writers and performers"– Provided by publisher.
Identifiers: LCCN 2020042580 (print) | LCCN 2020042581 (ebook) | ISBN 9781350155756 (paperback) |
ISBN 9781350155763 (hardback) | ISBN 9781350155770 (ebook) | ISBN 9781350155787 (epub)
Subjects: LCSH: Television comedies–Authorship. | Comedy films–Authorship. |
Comedy sketches–Authorship. | Playwriting.
Classification: LCC PN1992.8.C66 H43 2021 (print) | LCC PN1992.8.C66 (ebook) |
DDC 791.45/617—dc23
LC record available at https://lccn.loc.gov/2020042580
LC ebook record available at https://lccn.loc.gov/2020042581

ISBN: HB: 978-1-3501-5576-3
         PB: 978-1-3501-5575-6
         ePDF: 978-1-3501-5577-0
         eBook: 978-1-3501-5578-7

Typeset by RefineCatch Limited, Bungay, Suffolk
Printed and bound in Great Britain

To find out more about our authors and books visit www.bloomsbury.com
and sign up for our newsletters.

For **Kaia**, my youngest comedy student

Contents

Acknowledgements

I love having conversations about comedy and one of the great boons of writing books is the excuse it gives me to talk with a huge number of brilliant people about all things comedic. Once again my interviewees' generous sharing of their experience and insights have greatly enhanced the text. In order of appearance, my thanks go to the following: Steve Kaplan, Hollywood comedy guru, author of *The Hidden Tools of Comedy* and *The Comic Hero's Journey*; Ahir Shah, critically acclaimed and multi-award-nominated stand-up; Hopwood Depree, Los Angeles actor, writer, film producer and stand-up, currently based in the UK; Clelia Mountford, co-founder, with Sharon Horgan, of Merman Productions; John Gemberling and Neil Casey, Upright Citizens Brigade (UCB) improvisers, actors and writers; Steve Whiteley, actor, character comedian, writer, filmmaker and writer/director of international hit comedy short *Swiped* (2019); Katy Schutte, head teacher at Hoopla, co-artistic director of The Maydays and author of *The Improviser's Way*; Will Hines, UCB improviser, teacher and author of *How to Be the Greatest Improviser on Earth*; Lucy Lumsden, former BBC Comedy Commissioner and Head of Comedy at Sky TV, now boss of Yellow Door Productions; Daniel Audritt, stand-up and co-creator of Comedy Central's *Modern Horror Stories*; Robyn Perkins, stand-up and science comedian; Matt Parker, stand-up mathematician, one-third of Festival of the Spoken Nerd and author of bestselling book *Humble Pi: A Comedy of Maths Errors*; Richard Lindesay, stand-up and flute comedian; Pat Welsh, freelance workshop leader, senior lecturer and creator of the BA Comedy degree at Bath Spa University; Megan Salter, actor-writer and one-third of sketch group Muriel; Greg Buzwell, British Library curator of the Michael Palin archive; Kat Butterworth, writer/performer and co-creator (with the aforementioned Daniel Audritt) of *Modern Horror Stories*; Caitlin Campbell, improviser and artistic director of the Bristol Improv Theatre; and Rebecca MacMillan, improviser and teacher from The Maydays and Impromptu Shakespeare.

Thanks too to Marc Blake, Jonathan Broke, Tripp Crosby, Oliver Double, Roxy Dunn, Conor Jatter, Andrew Lanyon, Raphy Mendoza and Mike Orton-Toliver. And my heartfelt thanks once again to my stupendous wife, Kate Dineen.

Introduction

While putting the finishing touches to this book over a pot of fine green tea in the bar at Soho Theatre (a very civilized way to bring the writing to a close), I spotted a writer-performer whom I'd coached in scripting sitcom. I went over to say 'hi' and she was effusively apologetic about not being able to pin down a date for an interview. Now, it might appear perverse to introduce the book with talk of a non-interview, especially when there's an embarrassment of riches within from the interviews that did happen, including with one of her close collaborators. However, the reason we never found a date is itself instructive. She had been busy touring her extremely well received debut stand-up hour, acting in a forthcoming TV sitcom and writing sketches for a possible short-form comedy show on a new American app that promises to be a Netflix of bite-size shows for your phone. Before I went back to writing my book, and she to her meeting, as a down-payment on a future interview, she had this to say: 'Comedy is so competitive now, you have to do it all.'

Many of the comedy people I work with as director, script editor and teacher will indeed be doing it all. They'll be improvising, performing stand-up, writing sketches, making comedy to put online, filming shorts to enter into film festivals and writing sitcom scripts. It's that eclectic range of activity that has inspired this book, where the shortest comedy narratives discussed are one-liner jokes and the longest are sitcom and comedy dramas, alongside long-form improv and full-length stand-up shows. (In between these extremes are sketches, scenes and routines.) However, while the form and duration changes, the demands of narrative remain fundamentally the same: creating compelling characters, putting them in engaging situations, structuring the elements of your story and doing it all in your own distinctive voice.

It's these perennials of narrative that this book explores across the whole range of contemporary comedy. My aim, whether you're a specialist putting in the hours on one discipline or a multi-hyphenate Jaqueline-of-all-trades, is to enhance your comedy narratives, be they long or short, filmed or staged.

PART ONE

Inspiration

Chapter 1
The Comedy of Your Life

In my work as a comedy director, teacher and script editor, I work with many writers and writer-performers on developing narratives for sketches, short films, sitcom scripts, comedy drama, stand-up and more. If *you* are a writer-performer you're holding the right book, and you are just the kind of person the comedy industry is particularly interested in. If you're simply a *writer*, take heart. I'm sure you're confident, charming and charismatic, but I was speaking recently with a TV comedy producer who says in gatherings of comedy people she seeks out the quiet, withdrawn, awkward writers! (So maybe play down that charisma a bit.) As a writer, there's lots in this book for you, but if I may jump straight in with a big bit of advice for you, the writer, start performing too. If this is well outside your comfort zone, before you throw the book across the room (that'll cause a scene if you're browsing in a bookshop) – or less dramatically before you close the browser tab – I'm not suggesting you try and make a career of it. Just think of performing as a way to become a better writer. You could take some classes (stand-up, improv, acting, clowning) or at the very least start performing your scripts aloud with others. This will have a big knock-on effect on the naturalness and fluency of your dialogue and more.

Now, whatever form you're working in, the most immediate source of comedy is your own self and life experience. So, in this opening chapter we'll talk about your *comedic self*, the comedy persona that you present to audiences through your writing and performing, and the ways in which the raw ingredients of your life can be cooked up into comedy narratives. While your comedic self is present in all your work, the starkest and most immediate way to explore it is in stand-up, so we'll start from your persona in stand-up, making links with creating fictional characters. Full-length autobiographical stand-up shows then segue into autobiographical sitcom/comedy drama, which finally leads into improv in narrative comedy as another way of bringing your own self and voice into the work.

I regularly refer to the brilliant books of Hollywood comedy consultant Steve Kaplan, so I was cock-a-hoop to speak with him for this book. I began by asking him about the stand-up's persona and he told me, 'Stand-ups who are unsuccessful go out there and make comments about other people, just pointing their finger. Whereas a really good stand-up, like George Carlin, isn't just finding fault with others, he's creating a character who is expressing those thoughts, and at the same time you're laughing at him because he's the cranky old man. It's the persona that makes us laugh, not necessarily the nasty jibe or the observation. I think it's more important to write out of character than to come up with funny things to say or funny things to do. A good stand-up either takes the blame or shares the blame.'

In other words, you're either laughing at your own failings directly or acknowledging them alongside lampooning others. The majority of successful stand-ups share, laugh at and play with their negative sides. Kaplan says:

> It's important that whatever you do, you are in effect saying, 'I'm a fucked-up human being, but it's okay because so are you.' In a way, a comedian is like Jesus Christ because they are going to confess their sins for everybody else. You, the audience member, don't have to confess *your* sins, but here's why you're laughing: you know that this sin of the comedian's is also yours. But it's okay, you don't have to confess to the guy sitting next to you. The comedian will take it on for you.

The same is true in comedy screenwriting, where you can reveal the truth of your failings and embarrassments through the characters and situations you create.

Positives and negatives

In stand-up, then, what will make your comedy persona effective is drawing out and sharing your bad sides: your unskilful, shameful, embarrassing aspects. The good news from the point of view of your self-esteem is that to create a balanced persona, you need to show both negative and positive sides to the audience. All negative and you are so dislikeable as to turn the audience off. (Although there are outliers who can find an audience despite this.) All positive and it's very hard to find the funny. With a balanced persona, the positive things are why the audience will like you and the negative things are why they will find you funny.

Below is a table of 108 positive and 108 negative qualities. Ask someone you know well (and who will be relaxed and playful about doing this) to peruse this list and pick two positives and a negative for you. Even from a simple list of three words there are hints of the outlines of your comedic self. I recently asked my partner Kate to do this as an illustration of the exercise for a group, and for me she picked 'affectionate, decisive and impractical'. It's a fascinating exercise, as I wouldn't have picked these three for myself and after the warm glow of the two positives (and having sucked up the negative), I could now start working with these three attributes comedically. Try and find ways, as Tony Allen suggests in his book *Attitude*, of switching attitude; for instance, from positive to negative (and vice-versa). Say, for example, I am wanting to express affection for someone (positive), I could then go on to plan an entirely impractical way of doing it (negative). Or perhaps I am discussing some impractical solutions to a problem (negative) but then I could decisively pick one: a positive trait, but it won't be a positive outcome. Here we come to the interesting area where positive qualities cause problems, and misguided, impractical or simply insane methods to solve problems are at the heart of comedy.

To go deeper, pick three positives and three negatives, so you have a wider range of options to switch between. You will end up with something like this: *Courteous, Generous, Philosophical/Clingy, Impatient, Rigid*. If you're working on a character, as with your stand-up persona, the positive qualities will be why we like the character and the negative why we find them funny. When everything is going well for the character and they're comfortable, they will be manifesting their positive qualities. As soon as they are challenged, the negative will come out. Try writing a scene where they are attempting to get something they want from another character and are showing one or more of their positive qualities. Then as soon as they meet resistance, switch to one or more of the negative. The more pronounced and sudden the switches, the more vivid and comical a character will be.

A game you (or your characters) can play with the positives and negatives is to try to embody one or more of the positives but you keep being undermined and tripped up by one or more of the negatives. For example, I work with an improvisation exercise where you (or the character) are recalling a situation where you had to do something in your family life or in your relationship that was disagreeable but felt obliged to do it. The game is to try to talk about it generously and magnanimously, but for the bitterness and annoyance to keep slipping out around the edges. So, you're trying to project positivity but the negativity is nonetheless being communicated. This gap between what you're trying to project and what the audience perceive is where much character comedy is to be found. The bigger the gap, the bigger the potential comic value.

Positives		Negatives	
Accepting	Broad-minded	Aggressive	Bitter
Affable	Calm	Apathetic	Blunt
Affectionate	Candid	Arrogant	Boastful
Amiable	Careful	Authoritarian	Boring
Amicable	Caring	Belligerent	Bossy
Balanced	Charming	Bigoted	Callous
Brave	Cheerful	Bitchy	Careless

Continued

Positives		Negatives	
Communicative	Loving	Cheerless	Mean
Compassionate	Loyal	Clingy	Miserly
Conscientious	Lucid	Cold	Mistrusting
Considerate	Mature	Complacent	Moody
Convivial	Modest	Conceited	Narrow-minded
Cooperative	Motivated	Confrontational	Obstinate
Courageous	Open-minded	Controlling	Overcritical
Courteous	Optimistic	Covetous	Patronizing
Creative	Original	Cowardly	Pessimistic
Decisive	Passionate	Cowering	Petty
Determined	Patient	Critical	Pig-headed
Diligent	Persistent	Cruel	Pompous
Diplomatic	Philosophical	Cynical	Possessive
Discreet	Pioneering	Deceitful	Prejudiced
Devoted	Pleasant	Defensive	Pretentious
Dynamic	Plucky	Dishonest	Prideful
Easy-going	Polite	Disorganized	Quick-tempered
Elegant	Powerful	Dogmatic	Rebellious
Energetic	Practical	Ego-centric	Reluctant
Engaged	Pro-active	Egregious	Resentful
Enthusiastic	Punctual	Fearful	Rigid
Exuberant	Quick-witted	Finicky	Rude
Fair-minded	Rational	Foolish	Sarcastic
Faithful	Realistic	Fussy	Secretive
Fearless	Reliable	Greedy	Selfish
Friendly	Responsible	Grumpy	Self-satisfied
Flexible	Resourceful	Guarded	Small-minded
Focused	Romantic	Harsh	Sneaky
Forgiving	Self-confident	Hostile	Sour
Funny	Self-disciplined	Idle	Spiteful
Generous	Selfless	Immature	Stubborn
Gentle	Sensible	Impatient	Sullen
Grateful	Sensitive	Impractical	Suspicious
Gregarious	Sincere	Impulsive	Tactless
Hard-working	Sociable	Inconsiderate	Thoughtless
Hardy	Straightforward	Indecisive	Touchy
Helpful	Sympathetic	Indulgent	Unemotional
Honest	Thoughtful	Inflexible	Unpredictable
Humble	Tidy	Innocent	Unreliable
Imaginative	Tolerant	Insecure	Untidy
Impartial	Trusting	Insensitive	Untrusting
Independent	Understanding	Insincere	Untrustworthy
Intellectual	Unpretentious	Intolerant	Vague
Intelligent	Upbeat	Irresponsible	Vain
Intuitive	Warm-hearted	Jealous	Vulgar
Inventive	Willing	Lazy	Wasteful
Kind	Witty	Machiavellian	Weak-willed

Persona games

When working with comedy writers and performers, I often use improvisation in developing comedy characters and narratives, including with stand-ups as we explore their persona. Stand-ups will also improvise in performance, and all the more so in new material and work-in-progress shows. Indeed, a lot of comics feel they can only really 'write' on stage in front of an audience. Then there are stand-up nights where improv is an end in itself. I've recently been working with a comic who was due to take part in an improvised stand-up show where he'd be presented with topics and would be expected to ad-lib some material in response. It was to be his first attempt to improvise in front of an audience in this way, and despite being comfortable delivering material, this was a big step out of his comfort zone. I suggested to him that he go on stage with a number of 'games' in mind rather than going on stage with nothing, and having to pull something out of thin air when you see the topic. I suggested giving unhelpful advice to the audience, being inappropriately angry and being out of touch. Crucially my suggested list of games was based on attitudes I'd already seen him take in material that had worked with audiences. For example, he already has some funny material where he earnestly gives absurd advice to the audience, so it makes sense that this could be one of the games he has up his sleeve in an improvisational setting.

The first show of this kind that I saw was *Set List* at the Edinburgh Fringe in 2017. Still amongst the best of the improvised stand-up shows, *Set List* takes the form of a regular stand-up night with an emcee and a series of acts. The twist is that the acts go on stage with no knowledge of what they'll be talking about until a subject is flashed up on the screen behind them. Two of the topics on the night I attended were 'The Bill Cosby comeback tour' and 'Wheelie bin UBER'. The first of which led to some genuinely funny stuff, and the second, on the night, less so. The audience are happy to take the misses along with the hits however, as it's all part of the live, unpredictable nature of the night. Indeed, some comics got laughs by commenting on their failure. This is meta-comedy, where you self-referentially comment on the process of doing comedy.

At one point during the *Set List* show, a comic told the audience that he had an idea for a start-up business. He then turned round to discover the topic on the screen. It was 'domestic electric chairs'. He then riffed on this as his business idea. What the comedian had here was a game. He knew that whatever the topic, he'd frame it as a business idea. He got lucky in this case in that the idea readily fitted into the business frame. But it really doesn't matter if the subject is not a neat fit for a business. The more unlikely the subject is to be a business the better. What's more, applying a business mindset to subjects where it is a jarring fit could be brought to bear in written material too. For example, one could imagine this comic discussing the economic benefits of regularly phoning grandparents. In a *Set List* performance from 2014, readily findable online, the excellent Ahir Shah uses this device of putting a frame around the topic before he starts riffing on it. He begins by saying he's been in a mood all day, says 'Here's why' and turns around to see the topic – which turns out to be the 'Secret Agenda of Quakers'. The audience laugh at the idea that this is what has put him in a bad mood. He holds the mic close, and, in best conspiracy theory voice, asks 'Why are they always so fucking quiet?' Ahir described this approach to me as 'gaming the game'. He later goes into a lengthy, mock historical discussion that is funny, spontaneously in the moment, because it's coming through his established persona, tone of voice and point of view that has been built up over many, many hours of stage time.

Ahir Shah is a regular at *Set List*. When we talked for this book, I asked him about his experience of the show and he explained:

Although you are given some sense of structure by the topic that you're given, they're usually sufficiently vague to just be a vehicle for a comic expressing their own voice through this topic. When you have multiple people doing it over the course of a show, like proper sets you would have on a mixed-bill stand-up night, then you get the sense of, 'Oh, it really is conditional on the type of performer and the type of voice that we're listening to.' It becomes more interesting because of that. It's also a really fun one to watch as a comic. Because when you're on the balcony watching everyone else, we're all playing the game internally as well. You'll think, 'No, that's not what I would have done with that.' 'That's better than what I would have done with that.' Or, 'I couldn't get away with that but they can because of the way their persona works.' It really appeals to the nerdier side of the comic.

As a stand-up, to discover what games work best for you, review video of your stand-up gigs and try to identify the 'game' you're playing when things are working. Even better, ask someone to feed back to you. Improvisers and comedy actors can apply the same thinking to videos of their performances. Are you, for example, playing contrarian, short-tempered, misunderstanding, confused, horny, prissy, arrogant etc.? When writing stand-up, choosing a persona game to play with the topic you are working on can give you a head start. If, for example, you have a tendency to overthink things, a persona game might be to debilitate yourself ruminating on everything. If you have a short fuse in real life, a persona game could be to go ballistic over the slightest thing. If you have a tendency to awkwardness, a persona game could be to become the most inept, clunky person imaginable. A Rhod Gilbert game, for example, is being unreasonably angry; an Amy Schumer game is being shameless; a James Acaster game is saying something obscure and idiosyncratic but acting as if he believes we will find it relatable; a Jena Friedman game is playing innocent while being viscerally cutting; an Eddie Izzard game is describing something technical or historical without all the knowledge and terminology required. He fills in the blanks with whimsical speculation and surreal guesswork.

True stories in stand-up

When I spoke with Ahir Shah for my previous book he had just completed a trio of polemical shows. The focus was political with a personal thread. For his next show, *Duffer*, he'd turned this on its head: the show was personal with a political thread. It tells the story of his beloved grandmother, who when he was five was suddenly deported from the UK, and how he didn't see her until a trip to Gujarat reunited them twenty-two years later. While outwardly this change of direction from the political to the personal was a significant shift in his work, it all came about quite organically. Ahir told me:

> In the same way that with the previous shows the stuff that I was thinking about was the direction of the world in the era of Brexit and Trump, I couldn't get away from the fact that during that period [of developing *Duffer*] my thoughts were largely monopolized by certain stories from my family and things that were happening to us. It would have felt more forced to *not* talk about it that than it was to talk about it. I needed to talk about this stuff and the way that I talk about stuff *is* to an audience. That's why lots of people have said stand-up is like therapy; but you pay me rather than the other way around.

I asked Ahir about finding the comedy in such a sad situation and he said:

> By no stretch of the imagination was all of it funny when I started talking about it. I remember once during a preview about 40 minutes in someone just going, 'Oh God.' Okay, that's not what you want! Over time you work out the comic direction of it, you start placing this story you want to communicate into the form [stand-up] through which you communicate. My director Adam Brace was instrumental in making that happen.'[1]

Ahir said of sharing highly personal material in his stand-up:

> What's nice about it is the recognition of the extent to which stuff that can make you feel very alone is actually quite common. That everyone

---

[1] For more on finding the funny in personal pain, see chapter 12, 'Vulnerability and pain in stand-up shows', of my book, *A Director's Guide to the Art of Stand-up* (London: Methuen Drama, 2018).

feels very alone in their very common affliction. Therefore being able to, or attempting to, articulate it can be a very useful thing, not only for yourself but for people who will come up to you afterwards and say, 'Oh yes, that's how that works, I just never thought of it in those words.' I remember with *Duffer*, I was very, very reticent to discuss the fact that I'd considered euthanizing my grandmother. It was through discussing that with [the director] Adam that I realized that that's not a particularly uncommon thing in those sorts of instances. Then touring it around, talking about it, I lost count of the number of people who said to me, 'Yes, that was the thing that happened to me.' That was something that, for me, I felt very isolated in and felt like, 'Oh God, this is awful', that it was one of the worst thoughts or impulses that I'd ever had. But then you discover that actually it's a relatively common thing.

Ahir's next show, *Dots*, continued with this more personal direction. He told me that in the development process of *Dots* it originally ended on the sentiment, as he put it, 'Aren't I so happy and in love.' He went on:

Then that altered very suddenly, from my perspective. So, we're going really back to the drawing board here. There's not a huge amount of time in which to do that, particularly when you consider the amount of time that I spent entirely useless to the world. When it came to June, July [the Edinburgh Fringe is in August], I was like, 'Right, okay. This just needs to get out there [on stage] as much as possible and that's the way that we're going to be able to work it out.' Because everyone works differently but I'm definitely no good just sat in front of a computer typing stuff out. For me, it's much more about being able to do it in front of people.

As well as heightening aspects of yourself in your comic persona, the exact same thinking can be applied to other real people within your comedy. As Ahir puts it:

The familial character that I use most often, is my father. Everything is slight exaggeration. Something that my father would have said with 5 per cent tongue in cheek will instead be 100 per cent earnest just for the comic effect. It's always interesting talking about him because he rejects the characterization of him in my stand-up because he thinks he is considerably more normal than he actually is. Whereas all I have done is make him perhaps 10 per cent more weird than he is. In his mind, I have made him 1000 per cent more weird than he is. I certainly don't think that if anyone were to meet my mother or my father or my sister that they'd think, 'Oh God, this is entirely the opposite of the person he described.' They'd be like, 'Yes, I more or less got a sense of that.' That's an important thing in any sort of characterization. You should be able to make people feel like they know them.

Ahir took his father's presence in the show a step further in *Dots*:

> *Dots* ends with an audio recording of a conversation between me and my father about certainty. I'd gone through life thinking that my parents had it so worked out, and then right at the end of the show, you have this recording where he admits that in fact they didn't. I wrote it in a room with him because I didn't want to put words in his mouth. I wanted to express sincerely a way he feels. It's condensed conversations that we had. It's taking reality and having to condense it, shape it into a way that works as part of a narrative, while not wanting to lose the sincerity of the original emotion and intent. It was very important to me that he was part of that and that we were able to do that together. It felt nice to give him, maybe not the last word, but the penultimate word. Because really, every show is based on conversations that I have with my mother, my father, my sister, my closest friends. It just felt nice and correct to incorporate that in a more formalized way.

In 2019, I directed Hopwood DePree's true-story stand-up show *The Yank is a Manc! My Ancestors & Me*, which took in the Brighton, Manchester, Camden and Edinburgh Fringes. Hopwood has British ancestry and it was while idly researching his ancestry online in LA that he discovered he is heir to his family's then empty, derelict and crumbling stately home outside Rochdale named Hopwood Hall, which was built by his ancestors in the early fifteenth century. He sent an email to the local council in whose care the house was, and in return received some photographs from the council conservation officer. Discovering it was in desperate need of saving, he flew to Manchester to have a look. Despite it being a hard-hat zone, wrecked by time, the elements and vandals, enough of its magic survives and Hopwood fell in love with the place. In short order he'd left LA and relocated to the north of England on a mission to save the place, which raises the question, as he asks in the show, 'Can a guy from Hollywood make it in Rochdale?'

Working with Hopwood, the question that was uppermost in our mind throughout the process was 'How can the audience relate to this?' Hopwood recalled, 'Because it was an unusual circumstance, I really wanted the audience to relate. I felt the humour in any situation needed to be as universal as possible even though it really wasn't a universal situation. It felt important to try to find those stories or those events that hopefully people could see themselves in.' One approach was to bring it down to a scale that people could relate to, for example framing the restoration of the hall as 'the home renovation project from hell'. As Hopwood explained:

Most people can relate to putting in a new bathroom or maybe a new kitchen or a small extension. We wanted to make it so that it felt like that but times a thousand, so people could feel the sense of being overwhelmed. I even got overwhelmed back home in LA by doing one bathroom, and I said that in the show. In this project there's forty bathrooms plus all the rest of the building, the bedrooms and all the reception rooms and kitchens. The project is almost too daunting; it's so daunting that you just go numb.

There are many sides to Hopwood's character the story could highlight: bravery, spontaneity, generosity, imagination. But while the audience might warm to these positive qualities, they are not the stuff of comedy! It was clear that the comedy would come from Hopwood playing the fool, as he was already doing in video diaries he was making of his journey: 'I *am* the fool! And it's easier to play the fool than to play the intelligent one. It also, again, makes it more relatable for the audience. Everybody has walked into a new situation where you're feeling like you don't really fit in and you don't know what's happening and you feel like you're the fool.' The situations that most allowed Hopwood to show this fool side of his character were situations where he was a 'fish-out-of-water'. He said:

> I think that's relatable to most people whether it's at work or it's at school or in a new situation. Once we made that decision, we were looking for situations that could illustrate that fish-out-of-water experience. So it was a case of finding the central theme and then having everything else support that theme, and that's the through-line that runs throughout the whole show from beginning to end. If something wasn't supporting that, then it was easy to either say it should go, or to ask 'Is there a way we can tweak this story to make it support that central idea?'

Beyond Hopwood, there were a huge number of characters, in the present day and in history. Here it was very much the case of us doing all the things Ahir discusses. In Hopwood's words:

> You have to combine characters, situations and events to tell a story in a way that can be understood within 60 minutes. Most audience members like to follow a few specific characters. If you have ten or eleven people that have been significantly involved in the story, when you start to write it that way, you realize how quickly it becomes very confusing, and the last thing you want to do is lose your audience. You want it to be very simple in a way that people can follow along and sit back and enjoy the humour of it rather than trying to figure out who said what or who this character is. So three or four of them could be melded into one person, or three or four different incidents could be combined into one. At first, it's hard because you're saying, 'But, wait, this is a true story, this actually happened.' You have to let go of that.

The key character was gruff, Northern hall caretaker Bob. He'd heroically kept the hall (more or less) standing during the wilderness years. In the show, he and Hopwood's relationship became a Laurel and Hardy double-act. I asked Hopwood how it felt when Bob the caretaker actually came to see the show in Manchester: 'That was nerve-racking, to actually have the character from the show be there watching it! Bob even said of one moment, "Did I do that?" and I had to say, "No, but we based it on something else you did do."' Hopwood noted that despite some invention:

> We tried to stick with his voice and the types of things he would say, and to put us in the types of situations that I had been in with him, to make it still feel a very real story.

We did, for example, exaggerate the extent to which he took the mickey and the extent to which he was disdainful about America and Americans. There was some truth in that but it was really ramped up.

> Some of it was heightened or exaggerated for humour purposes, or for the telling of the story, but most everything was based on a kernel of truth.

For example, there is the story where it's Bonfire Night and Hopwood is hearing all these explosions but he has no idea what's going on. That much is true, but in the show it becomes Hopwood, terrified that it's World War III, ringing Bob who proceeds to wind him up that conflict has indeed broken out. This is *dramatic irony*. If you've studied Greek tragedy you'll be familiar with dramatic irony. It's where the audience know something that character(s) do not. So you have Oedipus unaware that the man he has murdered is his father, and the woman he is sleeping with is his mother; or in this example, Hopwood believes World War III is breaking out but we know it isn't. (Not yet anyway.) There's an extra time layer here, in that Hopwood as he's telling the story knows *now* about Bonfire Night, but he's going back and acting out the situation *then* when he didn't know. Dramatic irony can certainly fuel tragedy and it's a great device for creating comedy. It's a topic that threads throughout the book and we will go on to see examples in other kinds of comedy narratives.

From stand-up to sitcom

Aisling Bea is an actor, stand-up and writer who also draws on the truth of her life in her comedy, with versions of herself and her family featuring as characters. Having won the stand-up competition 'So You Think You're Funny' in 2012, Aisling returned to the Edinburgh Fringe in 2013 with her breakthrough hour

C'est La Bea. The heart of the show was about growing up in rural Ireland and, again, it's a heightened and edited version of the reality. From there she developed the comedy drama sitcom *This Way Up*, which took aspects of her life as an Irish woman in London and fictionalized them. The show was developed and produced by the powerhouse production company Merman, which was set up and is run by Sharon Horgan and Clelia Mountford. As a big fan of Merman's output, I was delighted to speak with Clelia. When we met, she told me, 'When we set up Merman in 2014, Sharon and I both wanted realistic, believable characters. We wanted to make people laugh and cry with our storytelling.'

The wonderful *Catastrophe* was an early hit for Merman. The show's writers and stars, Sharon Horgan and Rob Delaney, abided by one rule as they produced the scripts. In order to avoid cliché, they pledged to make nothing up. Horgan says that when she writes about experiences from her life, she connects to it more and has more to say.[2] Like Aisling Bea, Sharon and Rob are writer-performers. As Clelia says:

> With writer-performers, they hear their character already, or at least they've established some essence of their character in their stand-up and performance. With *Catastrophe*, Sharon and Rob could hear their characters as they're heightened versions of themselves. They stayed true to that. When they were writing, a lot of it was improvised in the room. They'd throw around dialogue, playing around with how the characters would react to certain situations. Once they'd found the voices of those characters, then it was about the story. What is this episode going to be about? What is this series going to be about?

Clelia said of this process, 'You need to understand exactly who that character is first and how they will react to certain situations, what their dynamic will be with other characters, what the backstory is. You can spend a lot of time doing that before anything goes into a script. You understand their world and what their thoughts are.'

I asked her how *This Way Up* came about and her answer provides an insight into the progression from idea to screen:

> Sharon and Aisling had written a slightly more heightened script about a woman who has a mental health issue. We've just made a pilot for HBO Max in the States. Before that it had been turned down by Channel 4 and as a result of that, Aisling went away and, rather than being discouraged, she sat down and wrote this new script, which was consistently original, about a

---

[2] T. Lewis, 'Sharon Horgan: "I want adventures. I want to do stuff that's challenging"', *Guardian*, 23 February 2020, https://www.theguardian.com/tv-and-radio/2020/feb/23/sharon-horgan-i-want-adventures-to-do-stuff-that-is-challenging.

woman who is in recovery. She wanted it to be hopeful and optimistic rather than about the actual breakdown. Aisling had written it as a vehicle for her and Sharon. Catastrophe was coming to an end at that point, and Sharon was very involved with script editing. Aisling trusts her and they go back years. They've written a film together in the past. She was in *Dead Boss* with Sharon. Sharon is very good at making cuts and going through in yellow highlighter on the page, and indicating 'You could get rid of this', 'You can condense that.'

Clelia told me that the show was originally called 'Sisters':

> . . . then it became 'Happy' and then 'Happy AF', but there were a lot of shows with similar names. So, we had to think again. Then Aisling was inspired by receiving a parcel that said 'This Way Up' and she felt that phrase reflected the hope and the optimism of the story she wanted to tell. In the early drafts, because she puts so much into her writing, there were lots of ideas and Channel 4 could see the potential. They then commissioned a second script. Quite often that happens. You get a two-scripts commission to see. And they wanted a 10-minute taster which we did. That was interesting in itself, crafting your taster around the two scripts to tell enough of the story. It was about 15 minutes in the end, to get a sense of the tone and how we wanted to shoot it. We shot her checking out of rehab and then that taster became the start of episode 1 when we got the series commission.

In *This Way Up*, Aisling's character Aine has suffered an emotional breakdown and the series charts her recovery. Aine gets through life with laughter and banter, and she'll come up with jokes to defuse situations, which Clelia tells me is very much how Aisling behaves too:

> There is the essence of Aisling's real self that runs through the character of Aine, so she had to make sure that it wasn't Aisling Bea performing and making sure her joking and banter was fully consistent with the character she was creating. In the edit she kept saying, 'That's Aisling. That's Aisling performing. That's not the character. Let's go for the more natural take.' She's a trained actress, she could see the difference. Aisling was all over the edit. She is an executive producer on it, it's very much her show. She wanted to be there and give notes and just make sure it was how she originally intended it to be. She saw it all.

As well as working on the script, Sharon Horgan acts in the show too:

> Sharon plays Aine's sister. Aisling actually has got a sister but she's very different from the one Sharon played. We have a duty of care to manage that.

That's why we help to create obvious distances between the characters and who they are based on. When people bring us their stories, I'm saying to them, 'Are you ready to put that on screen? How transparent do you want to be? Do you want to say "inspired by"? Do you want to dramatize it?' At the same time, what they're bringing in is so valuable and precious because it's based on truth and experience, and only they can tell that story because they've gone through it.

While a lot of *This Way Up* is inspired by her own life, Aisling wanted to make it more universal and write about other characters. As Clelia explains:

Aisling is an Irish immigrant living in London, and she writes about other immigrants through the language school [where Aine teaches], about how people are trying to make connections in different ways, and how people's definition of happiness varies from each other. She thought the language school was a nice way of having people away from home in a room together and trying to navigate the language and culture. That is the place where we see Aine at her happiest and we see she is good at her job rather than being a hot mess. Sharon and I find it difficult to engage with characters that are like that. We like to show female characters who are good at something, or achieving all they could be. That was important for us to show that she could communicate and reach out to people and help people as well. And to get into loneliness and immigration a little bit more there's the man who's lost his wife and is trying to make a connection with his French son who doesn't speak English that well, so again language is an issue.

Clelia went on:

Aisling knew she wanted to explore these themes. She knew she had her character of Aine. Then we had to reduce it because, in a good way, there was so much stuff there. You just try and home in on what each episode is about, and to make sure that it stayed true to the characters and tracking them across the six episodes. You only want a few core characters, because there are only so many you can have in 22 minutes and only so much you can do. Aisling made a plea at one point, 'Can we not have a 30-minute episode?' And I'd have to say 'No, they've got adverts to fit in!'

The end result was a show that people really responded to. As Clelia notes, 'Aisling was delighted by the response to *This Way Up* because people who were going through mental health issues found it so helpful and optimistic and encouraging. That's what you want really. People enjoy it but also take something from it. Sharon and I like to make things that make you think, that don't just make you laugh and entertain you, but also challenge you a little bit as well.'

Improv and writing

When working with writers, I always encourage improvisation in the writing process. Try ad-libbing the routine, speech or scene into your phone and then listen back for choice bits that can go into the script. Then when you have a draft of a script, you can return to improv to riff alternative lines. This tends to result in a truer, more flowing style of speech in the script. Clelia Mountford talked about Sharon Horgan and Rob Delaney improvising between themselves to feed into their scripts, but she told me that, 'Once it's a script, there's no improvisation on the set on the day because they're very exact in their dialogue. They've crafted those words.'

However, many contemporary sitcoms/comedy dramas *do* use improvisation during the actual filming too. For example, a sitcom where improv was integral to the production of the show was *Outnumbered*, by Andy Hamilton and Guy Jenkin. Commissioned by Lucy Lumsden when she was at the BBC, she told me that it was greenlit on the basis of a brief pitch that described how their concept was for a family sitcom where the children would improvise all their lines. In previous family comedies, children would speak lines written by middle-aged writers. On *Outnumbered*, thanks to the improv, the children actually speak as kids do. In production, the child actors were given an idea, an attitude, a few lines or some script before shooting a scene and, when the cameras were running, were free to ad-lib. Therefore, the adult actors playing the parents (Hugh Dennis and Claire Skinner) were constantly having to react to whatever the children felt like saying at the time, recreating the experience of real parents reacting to their kids.

Another show where improvisation produced the feel of the world in which the show was set was Armando Iannucci's heavily researched and meticulously crafted political comedy *The Thick of It*. Having the actors improvise mirrored the way the people they were playing have to think on their feet, deal with unexpected crises and improvise policy on the hoof. Writers were brought into the process, including Jesse Armstrong, co-writer of *Peep Show* and co-creator of *Succession*, who has a background in politics. The plotting process was done with Armando Iannucci and the writing went back and forth with him until rough-and-ready, open-ended scripts were produced that Iannucci intended to be improvised around. The actors familiarized themselves with the scripts but didn't learn them, so there was a freshness and spontaneity to the performances, giving the show a naturalistic, documentary feel. Each episode was constructed in the edit from around 90 minutes of material, with Iannucci cutting any lines that were too obviously comedic to preserve the reality of the world. *The Larry Sanders Show* was a big influence on Iannucci, with him describing *The Thick of It* as a cross between *Sanders* and *Yes Minister*.

Improvisation is an increasingly common tool in the writing and production of scripted (or part-scripted) comedy. Casting is central in this kind of process, as the characters come to be very much moulded around the people who play them; character as a 'thin veil' over the performer. Indeed, there are many examples of partly improvised sitcoms where the characters literally *are* the performer; a classic example being Larry David in *Curb Your Enthusiasm*, alongside Ted Danson and others who appear as a comedic version of themselves. In *Curb*, an episode's plot is carefully constructed and written up as an outline, but the actors improvise the lines in each scene across multiple takes captured by two cameras, the best bits of which are painstakingly stitched together in the edit to make the final scene. This approach came about because latterly on *Seinfeld*, the actors knew the characters so well that Larry David felt they would need only to be told the situation and they could play out the dialogue themselves and ultimately David was able to work in this way on *Curb*.

Even when there is a conventional script, improvisation can be used to supplement and enhance the written material. The Comedy Central sitcom *Broad City*, created by and starring Ilana Glazer and Abbi Jacobson, draws closely on their real selves as it's based on their real-life friendship and their attempts to make it in New York. They have a background at the Upright Citizens Brigade improv school and theatre (UCB) and improvisation informed the process of making the sitcom. The show was produced using a writers room process, with Glazer and Jacobson acting as showrunners. Most of the writers in the room had a performance background, and were playful and open to ad-libbing and so sometimes the two protagonists would act out a situation and the writers would improvise the other characters. The best of this spontaneous material would find its way into the scripts. So that's the first point at which improvisation informed the process.

Secondly, whilst they did then shoot the carefully crafted script, typically once they'd filmed two or three scripted takes, they'd then invite the actors to improvise a take in their own words, and some of the improvised flourishes would be included in the final edit. The gross yet loveable character of Matt Bevers in *Broad City* is played by improviser, actor and writer John Gemberling of UCB. When we spoke, John explained to me, 'With Broad City, we were all friends, Abbi, Ilana and I, and they specifically wanted me to play that character. They wrote it to my strengths as a performer and for me it was less creating a character and more just tapping into the slob that I know how to be in my life. It comes naturally to me!' There's a link here with a stand-up amplifying unattractive parts of themselves. Regarding the improvisation side of it John told me, 'That show was fun to improvise on because the writing is good to begin with, and then there's space to improvise. It gives everything a more natural quality.'

John's friend and fellow UCB improviser, actor and writer Neil Casey also appeared on the show. Neil told me, 'I often get called in to play a straight man who gets upset, doing a Gene Wilder turn. My favourite one to play is the accountant on *Broad City* where I love straight-manning. I don't mind never having a joke. I like playing it totally deadpan.' Whilst *Broad City* was a positive experience of marrying script and improv, both John and Neil felt this process is often not so well handled. Like many improvisers, Neil is wary of being asked to improvise on camera in a scripted show: 'As a process, I don't particularly enjoy improvising when the camera's rolling, I mean, if I'm inspired or asked to, I'll certainly do it, but I think the best process is to let actors play with the material and improvise in rehearsal and then on the day, generally stick to the script.' As John remarked, 'It is forced a lot of times when they're like, "you're an improviser, so now improvise on camera". But then I'm wondering: can my scene partner improvise? Is there something to improvise *about*? A lot of times, improvising on camera just means, "come up with alternatives to the lines".' There's a lot of pressure there for the improviser to come up with the goods, which is felt even more acutely if there's a sense that the material is not there in the script.

Done well, however, the marriage of improv and script can elevate the production. If you're planning on filming some comedy, maybe a taster for a sitcom, a web series (and *Broad City* started as a web series) or a comedy short, improvisation could well be part of the process. Consider each of these approaches in turn as to how it could serve your project:

1   Use improv to feed into the script, which is then shot as written.

2   Film the scripted scenes as written and then also do improvised takes of the same material, so that the final product is a blend of script and improv.

3   Produce a script that acts as a guide and the actors are free to disrupt and improvise around in filming.

4   Write a story only, with no written dialogue. All the scenes are improvised. Construct the finished scenes from multiple takes in the edit.

I particularly like option 2, the *Broad City* approach. Key & Peele's sketches are also created through a mix of improv and writing, with for example an idea that develops in improv becoming a written script that then gets improvised around on the day of shooting and constructed into its final form in the edit. Steve Whiteley, with whom I worked on the comedy short *Swiped* (2019), used exactly this approach, with the final edit being a mix of scripted and improvised lines, but we absolutely wanted the script itself to be honed so we were not lazily reliant on the spontaneity of the actors on the day. Steve told me, 'I'm fully aware that a lot of the time what comes out of an actor's mouth in the spur of the moment is going to be far funnier than what I could ever think of writing. I'm a big believer in it, but I'm also a big believer in getting the script done to the best of your ability and then allowing for those moments of improv on the shoot.'

I also like to work with this approach in a range of contexts beyond filming. For example, a comic's stand-up routine will often evolve in this way too, beginning quite freely extemporized, then edited and honed, and finally in performance left with some openness for spontaneity. And at the time of writing, I'm directing actor, improviser and Free Association improv teacher Jonathan Broke in *Chum*, a one-man character comedy show where he plays a smooth, privileged politician who, during the book launch for the first volume of his memoirs, unexpectedly turns into a dog (yes, you did read that right). He has drawn on aspects of himself for the role, giving the character his own Norfolk background and taking inspiration from his own experiences. Our sessions together feature a lot of improvisation, which Jonathan records, and this then feeds into the script he's writing which will itself have space for further improvisation in live performance. He told me:

> I recognize that my strength as an improviser is in creating a relationship between me and my scene partner, and then heightening the comedy through listening and playing. In that area I feel most alive and most creative. So, when instead I choose to sit down, on my own, with a pen and paper and hope to write a script that's as funny as a spontaneous scene with another person, I am often disappointed about how pedestrian and familiar my thoughts are. For me, the access to my creative and comedic palate comes through bouncing ideas off a skilled director, who knows how to take the conversation in a direction that supports the overall journey of the character. This way I can find things that are more surprising to myself and the whole project gathers pace. That's what I've found in our sessions, we get a lot done, and fast, because there is fun to be had in playing with the ideas before they are scripted. Also, the characters I tend to play, and especially in *Chum*, are authority figures who are reactive, not proactive, through complacency. So, having someone to react to is really the only way to find the character!

Finally, I asked UCB improvisers John Gemberling and Neil Casey how improv has informed their own scripted comedy work. John told me:

> I think doing improv allows you to think on your feet *when writing*. I feel like it's helped me with writing dialogue; gaming out what people would say and having it be funny and natural and also, heightening ideas. A lot of times in improv, you'll be like, 'We've got to heighten the idea' and then you end up

doing something too ridiculous. Whereas sitting down and writing, you can stop and think, 'Maybe that's too ridiculous. Let's pull it back. Here's a more reasonable way to heighten it.' I don't think most people that write start in improv necessarily, but I think it's an interesting tool to have. For example, when writing a scene: a scene should *be a scene* and not just a vehicle for moving a plot forward. I mean, you certainly watch a lot of TV and movies where there is no point to a scene except to be say something like, 'The email is encrypted and we have to go over here to get the thing.' It's just moving the plot along. I think the simple notion that any scene you do should have, for lack of a better word, a game that then can be heightened is an interesting one.

Neil added, 'When you're trying to write a sketch, [as an improviser] you've got good instincts for how to get to the important facts and stick to what's funny. With writing, the improviser's sense is that you can make it pretty good pretty fast and get it over the line and out the door. Also, the understanding from improv that everything is ephemeral can be a nice counterbalance to any inclination to be really precious about your ideas or to get hung up on things.'

In this opening chapter, we've considered the many and varied ways your own self and life experience can inform your writing and performing. It can be cathartic and liberating to take the more shameful, embarrassing, unskilful or unpleasant aspects of your life and transmute them into comedy. Improvisation too can be a great tool to take you past the censoring or overcritical mind to grow truer and more spontaneous dialogue and action from the soil of your experience. In the next chapter, we turn our gaze outwards to all the comically dysfunctional and idiosyncratic people in the world around us as we explore how they too are the stuff of comedy.

Chapter 2
People Watching

Naturalistic Chicago improvisers TJ & Dave will walk on stage with no opening line, emotion, point of view or character ideas. How, then, do characters and narrative emerge? Their whole approach is based on paying close attention to your scene partner who, they say, will give you everything you need. They will spend time at the opening of a show just observing each other. The TJ & Dave approach calls on you to be minutely attentive to, and fully present with, your scene partner to pick up on subtle cues. For instance, if you look closely, your partner will have some energetic or emotional quality, some kind of look in their eyes, a physical attitude, a close or a distant proximity. They also talk about perceiving the 'heat' and the 'weight' between you. The heat is the emotional intensity from cool and distant, to hot and intimate. The weight is how serious the issue at hand is, how 'heavy' the topic, from trivial to profound. They urge us to not impose something on the situation, to not drop in an outlandish idea from nowhere. Respond to what is actually at hand, they say. In responding to the information you receive from each other, the dynamic changes and so characters and a narrative are built, step by natural step.

Improviser Katy Schutte (of Hoopla and The Maydays) has performed improvised shows in this realist, highly present and attentive vein with Rachel Blackman, as Katy & Rach, for over a decade. My own work with improvisation is of a means-to-an-end kind. Basically, I use improv to get somewhere else: to a character, a sketch, a script, a bit of stand-up, a whole show. So, it's always a great learning experience for me to talk to people, like Katy, for whom (as Del Close originally championed) improv is an end in itself. When we spoke, Katy told me:

TJ & Dave is the touchstone for this slow-burn, naturalistic 'speed of life' type of improv and I've been very lucky to work with them a few times and Katy & Rach was inspired by their style. Silence and subtext are important. You have to be comfortable enough on stage to shut up and be present. You'll use truth a lot. You'll be honest and confessional and you'll be up for sharing; in the same way that very good stand-up is confessional. But unless you're saying 'We're going to do a monologue that is true', the audience won't know; you could be saying stuff that's absolutely private and personal, and people would just assume it's made up for the character. There's a safety in that.

TJ & Dave are working across an hour in a long-form show, patiently building a narrative and not overly concerned with when (or even if) it starts to become funny. Doing scene work with a sketch energy, however, is a different discipline. Then you need to be focused on finding the funny quickly. I have been particularly influenced by the work of the Upright Citizens Brigade (UCB), whose approach is tailor made for this, so I was very pleased to speak with Will Hines of the UCB Theatre in Los Angeles for this book. In terms of character creation, in the UCB approach, they will encourage you to enter a scene having made a definite choice beforehand. Will told me:

> I usually start with either a voice or body language, and you don't totally know what kind of person is going to result from that. You maybe change your body, pop out your chest, come in very confident. And then you figure out the rest. With the voice, it's not like an accent or a cartoon voice, just an attitude, a personality in the voice; it could be frightened and shy, or confident and loud. Then depending on how the other person responds, you start to flesh it out from there.

I asked Will how much of himself is in the characters that he improvises on stage and he told me:

> For me personally, a tremendous amount. I would say I'm 90 per cent of everybody I am, but that's not so true for everybody. Some people change much more into different people. I'm mostly me, and I adjust as needed. It's the angry version of me, it's the shy version of me. I start very much with what would I say in this situation. I think it's like being a good liar. You try to lie the minimum that you need, otherwise it gets you in trouble. That way I have less to manage. I think that still gives you quite a range. The version of me when I'm in love and dazzled, and trying to please somebody, is quite different than the version of me who's scared about running out of money. We contain multitudes.

I also spoke with Will's fellow UCB improvisers, actors and writers John Gemberling and Neil Casey, who we met in the first chapter. John recalled doing this exercise with teacher Michael Delaney at UCB: 'It was a great exercise that I never forgot. The idea is before you start a scene, you change your body position. For example, lean in so your centre of gravity is different. It immediately informs your character.' Neil recalled,

I remember that exercise too. I do that now. When you improvise, when something's about to start, you look at the other person, then you just walk in with something physical. Even if it's just a slight physicality it'll inform the whole thing somehow. I always think about that in terms of how I observe the world too. Like you'll see somebody and notice 'That person walks, leans back or walks on their tiptoes'. It's good. It taught me how to look at people. You can tell a lot about a person just from their posture. How their jaw's set or something like that.

You can also work with voice and physicality in comedy writing. When you're scripting your character, drop into their physicality. At the laptop, take on the way that they hold themselves, adopt their energy, and start typing their lines from there. And the voice? I'm a great believer that in writing dialogue you want to be speaking it as you write. Okay, this approach is harder in a cafe but you can subtly change your physicality, and at least mutter the lines under your breath. Who cares if you look a little crazy? Even better, put aside the laptop and improvise dialogue into your phone. Then when you come to edit and transcribe it, it'll have a naturalness and spontaneity that's hard to achieve just typing into a laptop. When you're creating a character in a script, in your early exploratory drafts you can write like an improviser too. Leap in first with big, clear decisions, bubbling up from we know not where, and then start to figure out the story of who the character is and why they acted that way. Work out the story they tell themselves and others. And then, because you are the omnipotent controller of these people's lives, you can figure out the story they don't even know themselves.

Observation of people

As a comedy writer and performer, you are an observer of people and of life. John Gemberling told me:

> I'm constantly writing down notes. I don't use most of them directly in stuff that I write, but I can't help it. If I see somebody that's interesting, or have a thought or a take on something that I think is interesting, I'll usually write it down; or mean to write it down and get upset if I forget what it was! If you observe people, behaviour, posture and mannerisms enough, it sinks into your subconscious so that when it is time to perform or create a character, that stuff is just in there. Occasionally, I will see somebody truly behaving insanely and I'll go, 'I've got to write that down!' It's such an interesting way to be in the world.

Fellow actor-writer-improviser Neil Casey said:

Tapping into your observations of real people out there in the world, synthesizing your work as an actor, writer or improviser with your experiences is inevitable. I sometimes see myself playing some stuff on video and I can pick up who I'm ripping off. Sometimes it's John! I'll generally have a notebook or some other recording medium where I'll be jotting down ideas or something really crazy I've seen. The more you pay attention to that process and are intentional about what you store in your utility belt, I think the better you can do. Then when I have a writing deadline, I'll go back and browse through that stuff.

Basing characters on real people you observe in life gives them a surer foundation than simply making someone up. You might base a character on someone close to you, your nearest and dearest, as we discussed in the opening chapter. However, if you're basing a character on someone you know less well, or even have only seen fleetingly, there's a lot you don't know and you are free to invent to fill in the gaps. Moreover, you don't feel any obligation or loyalty to them, allowing you to do them more of a disservice. If you don't have a real-life model (or models) in mind, you are more likely to draw on stereotype and cliché. Real people of course *can* actually be stereotypes, like the xenophobic cab driver I had the other day. But they have their own quirks and idiosyncrasies that take them beyond the stereotype. My cab driver also played loud opera in his car, so if he is my starting-point for my xenophobic cabbie then I'm getting a richer character than one I'd simply made up from a hazy stereotype, especially if I blend him with an Irish cab driver I had recently who switched back and forth from chatting cheerfully with me to shouting aggressively out of the open window at other motorists.

Aware that cab drivers have been a staple topic of stand-up comedians over the years, I thought I'd search on YouTube to find the latest such material. In a sign of how stand-up is taking off in India, at the top of the listings was a high-octane performance from a young, slight and yet powerhouse stand-up from Mumbai, Urooj Ashfaq. Her set about Uber drivers in her city has, at the time of writing, over five million views. It's fascinating to watch as her energy is compelling and I found it followable despite not all of it being in English. She begins with observations from her experience of using Ubers and then at the heart of the piece is a story of a driver assuming she's Hindu (she's actually Muslim), and she plays along to hear how he will rant about Muslims. (It's *dramatic irony* in that we the audience know that she is Muslim but the cab driver doesn't.) It's a specific driver in an actual situation which lifts it out of commonplace observations about the noxious opinions of cab drivers. It's also a textbook illustration of how to do an act-out. She deftly moves from framing the situation for the audience to casually and immediately dropping into the character of the driver in dialogue with her. There is a whole sequence of such act-outs across the piece illustrating how stand-up is peppered with these micro-sketches.

In sketch comedy, many of the most memorable characters of recent times have been created by Catherine Tate. She brings to her characterization proper acting credentials, including spending a year with the Royal Shakespeare Company before turning to comedy. She was part of Lee Mack's Perrier Award nominated *New Bits* show at the Edinburgh Festival Fringe in 2000 and returned to the festival the following year with her own one-woman show which ultimately led to her BBC TV sketch series. In recent times I've collaborated with Lucy Lumsden. As the first Controller of Comedy Commissioning at the BBC, Lucy was responsible for commissioning shows such as *Outnumbered*, *Miranda*, *Gavin and Stacey*, *The Thick of It*, *The Trip*, *Nighty Night*, *Rev*, *Lead Balloon* and more. More recently she's shifted to the role of producer and set up her own independent production company, Yellow Door Productions. Lucy, who commissioned *The Catherine Tate Show* for the BBC, told me,

> Catherine started with the Edinburgh show and then she worked up a few key characters with Geoffrey Perkins at Tiger [Aspect], and then a showcase was put on at Shepherd's Bush Theatre as a read-through. She was eight months pregnant at the time! She got commissioned right there and then. It was all very simple. I don't even remember much in terms of costume or wigs or anything. She just had all of those characters really clearly drawn. It was expertly done with a huge amount of confidence and great timing.

One of Catherine Tate's most celebrated characters is Nan, who Tate describes as a belligerent old lady (noting that basically all her characters are belligerent and don't like the world). Nan is based on a real person. When Tate was at drama school she was sent out as part of a group of four to old people's homes to give the residents a 'trip down memory lane'. However, they soon found that, 'old people can't be dragged down memory lane'. Dressed in old fashioned clothes and hats, they prepared a repertoire of songs pensioners would recognize from their youth. Tate says that at one place in north London, a no-nonsense elderly Londoner said in response to their spirited performance (in what was to become Nan's voice), 'Is she gonna stand in front of that fucking telly all day?'[1] Of course, Tate's experience of this woman was fleeting, but it's that lack of knowledge about the person that can really open up the space to be creative. Another great example is the grotesque character of Tubbs, who in *The League of Gentlemen* runs the local shop with Edward and is forever fearful of incomers and the threat they pose to the 'precious things of the shop'. The character has its origins in a certain Mrs Briggs who owned a quaint little gift

---

[1] 'Catherine Tate reveals the inspiration for Nan', interview with Catherine Tate, *The Graham Norton Show* (TV programme), BBC1, 21 October 2016, https://www.youtube.com/watch?v=LQco8BM1DuQ&t =3s.

shop in the Lanes in Brighton, and one day happened to feel fearful of the high-spirited Gents who were in the shop at the time of their debut shows at the Kommedia in Brighton. That fleeting interaction was blown up into a truly monstrous character. As Steve Pemberton says, you get the kernel of an idea and you run with it and expand it.[2]

'As if'

I asked Lucy to pick a favourite Catherine Tate character and she chose her Posh Mum, which serves as a good example of the 'as if' comedy approach which I refer to often in my work and throughout this book. Tate plays a recognizable middle-class metropolitan mother with all the concerns and pretensions of that kind of person, but blown up to an insane pitch. For example, at the children's school sports day in the egg-and-spoon race it's discovered that the eggs aren't organic and there is screaming, terror and a stampede *as if* in a horror movie. A later sketch features the family's Land Rover Voyager going in for a service and the family having to use a hire car instead: 'a car that other people have been in!' the children cry out, aghast. The mother delivers the news to the children with pure terror and when the (nonplussed) working-class man from the garage brings them the car he is treated *as if* he's a terrifying threat to the family. This kind of mother might be quietly 'horrified' at some of these things, but the game is blowing it up to horror movie proportions. Lucy recognized the kind of person the character is based on: 'Of course, for me, I knew quite a lot of mums a bit like that. So, there's a pleasure where it's a little mirror to my world. It's a little satirical nod to something I know really well.' Tate revisits this character across a sequence of sketches, each time playing the game in a different way. Lucy adds, 'Catherine was really, really good at that. I picked out that one but there were so many like that. Very simple, repeated ideas. There's such pleasure in the repeated idea and much of the enjoyment is the anticipation of what's to come.' Even though as a viewer you know where it's going, there's still an element of surprise: 'You're not quite sure how it's going to manifest itself.'

Tate's Posh Mum reacting with terror to everyday situations that offend her sensibilities reminds me of the Key & Peele sketch 'Flicker', where a trivial and childish office dispute plays out *as if* it's an intense psychological drama in a thriller. This notion that someone is behaving *as if* they were in another context or situation is a useful comic shorthand. When we spoke, Will Hines gave me an example of how it might play out in improv:

---

[2] 'The Original "Local" Shop – Comedy Map of Britain', documentary with Steve Pemberton, *Comedy Connections*, BBC2, 19 May 2008, https://www.youtube.com/watch?v=eQkjXPzx2zs.

The scene is an intervention, but instead of trying to get someone to quit drinking, you're trying to get them to stop taking selfies. It's got all the gravity and sombreness of trying to get someone to quit drinking, but I'm applying it to their Instagram strategies. The tone doesn't totally fit the situation, and therefore is funny. Sometimes we call that a 'mapping scene'. I'm taking an intervention and mapping it onto Instagram stuff.

When we spoke, Steve Kaplan talked with me about a scene from *Seinfeld* that he discusses in his seminars, where Jerry and George are in the back of a police car: 'They're in the back of a cop car and they're fighting with each other. I ask people, "Who and what are they acting like?" They say, "They're acting like kids in the back seat of a car." You can make it as crazy as you want as long as it adheres to some sort of reality.' Steve calls this a metaphorical relationship. This is the idea that beneath the surface relationship there is another informing it. He went on:

I'll then say, 'Okay, how many of you have kids?' Some of them raise their hands. I ask, 'How many of you *were* kids?' Everybody raises their hand. What metaphorical relationship does is it takes the onus away from making shit up and take you into recollection. A metaphor replaces something surface and maybe stale, with something that's real and personal. So rather than talking about generic kids in the back seat of a car, 'How did *I* act with my brother in the back seat of a car?' Then it became personal. Ultimately all fiction is autobiography.

Or to put it another way, Jerry and George are behaving *as if* they are kids.

Characters based on famous people

The beauty of characters based on people the audience have never met is you can use them as a springboard to create a more extreme, imaginary character. When your character is an impersonation or a caricature of someone the audience *will* know, someone famous, then part of the pleasure for the audience is you getting them right. I asked Neil Casey about writing sketches for *Saturday Night Live* and other topical, satirical shows: 'Everybody expects caricature from sketch. As a writer, you don't really have much of a responsibility to give a holistic portrayal of the people that you're satirizing because that's not really the point of satire. You're going to home in on the thing you're trying to make fun of, or the comedic angle that you're trying to take, and then work backward from there to how the character is going to be.' Let's take Tina Fey's celebrated portrayal of Sarah Palin on *Saturday Night Live* as an example. You will recall that in his presidential race against Barack Obama, John McCain picked the Alaskan governor as a running mate to offset his old, establishment image. She was considered folksy, down-to-earth and relatable. With Sarah Palin, the main writer Seth Meyers and Fey are making the point that she is out of her depth and parochial, which chimes with how people saw her. When she developed her version of Sarah Palin, interestingly Tina Fey did not simply pore over videos of the real person. While she did pay close attention to Palin's accent and her particular tone and vocal emphasis, working hard to place her voice regionally, she also drew on people she knew; for example, a friend's mother who had a similar tone.[3]

John Gemberling meanwhile played Steve Bannon, Donald Trump's chief strategist in the early days of his presidency, on Comedy Central's *The President Show*. I asked him how he approaches the performance when he's playing an actual person the audience know:

> I did it with John Belushi in *A Futile and Stupid Gesture*, John Hancock in *Making History* and Steve Bannon. With a straight acting role, you're supposed to take on the perspective of the character you're playing, whether it's a real person or not. With someone like Steve Bannon on *The President Show*, the premise of the show is 'these people are awful ghouls' so it's a different approach and the fun of it is in showing your disdain through how you portray them. It's a heightened version, because when you watch Steve Bannon, aside from the fact that he looks like he's fucking melting, he doesn't actually act that crazy in most circumstances. I studied Steve Bannon: he has a slight Southern twang, and he's just a straight-talking guy who's saying insane things. I drew from him as much as I could, but then I have my own idea of what this guy is like when not on camera, as evidenced by the fact that his clothes are rumbled and filthy. He looks like he fell asleep in the sun on a bench. I made up my own picture of him as the slobbering demon he becomes as soon as the camera turns off; he's a stumbling drunk at sixes and sevens, slurring his words and tumbling down the stairs. That's what I was playing.

When working with a person in the public eye, ask yourself what is the perception, how do people see this person? Then what are you highlighting and what point are you making? Exaggerate the aspect of them you want to criticize. Another way to work with a famous person is to put them in the world of your fictional show. I'm not suggesting that they visit or drop in – simply relocate them and rename them, turning them into a fictional character. You might take, for example, Tony Blair, rename him Toby Bancroft and make him the owner of the deli in your sitcom. You don't even need to tell anyone Blair is your inspiration. And given you are not looking for laughs of recognition, you can take all sorts of liberties building up the

---

[3] 'Tina Fey On Sarah Palin Impression', interview with Tina Fey, *David Letterman Tonight*, CBS, 19 May 2008, https://www.youtube.com/watch?v=GBAqGSbPwkQ.

character from this Blair basis, to a degree that people might not even make the connection but you've given yourself a solid foundation. And even if they do notice, it becomes part of the enjoyment: 'Toby is a little Tony Blair'. This approach immediately gives you a vivid character and a voice you can hear in your head as you write. Another way of getting an immediate voice in your head for your character as you write is to imagine a famous actor playing the role. On an online Writing Narrative Comedy course I am teaching at present, one of the students, as she writes, imagines Greg Davies playing her central character. Even if she's never lucky enough to land Davies for the role, having him in mind means she can vividly hear and see the character. As you write, you might even picture completely unobtainable Hollywood A-listers playing your characters – or deceased Ealing Comedy actors!

Use their own words

When working with a person from real life you don't need to invent things for them to say. Your starting-point can be their own words. As Fey observed, a lot of the material Seth Meyers wrote for her to perform as Sarah Palin was based around things she had actually said. Back in the 1960s satire boom, Peter Cook was impersonating the prime minister of the day Harold Macmillan. The real Macmillan was the last of his kind: learned, patrician, patriarchal. For audiences of the day it was breathtaking to hear the prime minister being impersonated. It was as recently as the 1950s that the age of deference still held sway and the PM would be off-limits for comedy. Indeed, when Peter Sellers wanted to impersonate Winston Churchill for *The Goon Show*, a nervous BBC only agreed on the basis that the impression would be entirely respectful and would not say anything contentious. And yet by the 1960s in *Beyond the Fringe*, Cook was viciously lampooning the PM even while he was sitting in the audience watching the show in the west end of London (to the horror of his fellow cast members). And like Tina Fey many decades later, he based his impersonation around the prime minister's own words.

Their own words can create laughs of recognition for the audience, particularly in an edited and heightened form that play up the aspects of them you're wanting to satirize. Another approach is to use their original words as a set-up and then you add a payoff. Here are some examples from Peter Cook that use Macmillan's words as set-ups with Cook's added afterthoughts (spoken in character) in bold. This is speaking the subtext – or as I say, it's the 'unsaid said'. He is made to literally say the things that would normally go unspoken. You put in their mouth the very criticism you want to make:

I have recently been travelling the world on your behalf . . . **and at your expense**.

Britain is a sometime honest broker in the world. No nation could be more honest. **No nation could be broker.**

There are people in the world a lot less well off than you . . . **and it is the policy of the Conservative party to ensure that position is maintained**.

A notorious twenty-first-century equivalent of Peter Cook lampooning the prime minister who sat in the audience is stand-up Michelle Wolf fearlessly eviscerating members of Donald Trump's administration at the White House Correspondents' Dinner, where many of her targets were actually sitting in the room listening to her. And as Cook did, she also used the president's own words in her routine which, needless to say, were of a very different tone to the considered and genteel remarks of Harold MacMillan.

To try this, pick a person in the public eye that you have a strong opinion about. Starting from a position of anger can drive the comedy but equally you might actually feel some affection for the person but you can still see their foibles and failings. Get some actual words of theirs. Maybe find the text of a speech they made or transcribe some of their words from an online video. When you have some text of their speech, now you can set about adding in your own afterthoughts.

Using the words the actual person spoke can work just as well with people known only to you and not to the audience: for example, Peter Cook's character of E. L. Wisty, a nasal droning oddball bore, was based on a Mr Boylett who was a table butler at Radley College, Cook's (obviously very posh) school. At school, Cook would impersonate Mr Boylett and subsequently used him as a character on stage, changing his name. Apparently the real Boylett came out with bizarre notions such as his claim that he'd seen various inanimate objects move and was now attempting to sell them for a fortune. Cook would put Boylett's utterances straight into his performance and then, building on the template provided by the real person, would write even more absurd lines in the same vein.

Character motives and transposed behaviour

Returning to the theme of improv as a writing tool we discussed in Chapter 1, when I wrote sketches with the founder of Angel Comedy, Barry Ferns, including for live shows *Doreen* and *The Leisure Virus* twenty years ago, most of our ideas emerged from hanging out and riffing on comic concepts that came up in conversation. Will Hines recognized this: 'My first draft is always essentially improvised, either solo or with a friend. Then I just go back and try to tighten it up. I don't know any other way to do it.' At one point when we spoke, Will started exploring the kind of behaviour you might exhibit if you're overly solicitous. He said, 'You worry about the people in the room. You put cushions underneath them, you ask if they need a glass of water.' This could be the perfectly functional behaviour of a thoughtful host, but it starts to become comic when it's excessive or unwelcome – for example, Mrs Doyle in *Father Ted* foisting endless cups of tea on people. Another way of making the behaviour comic is to transpose it to an unlikely context. I suggested to Will for the overly solicitous character that 'they're in a foxhole and it's a firefight in a war'. Will ran with this and ad-libbed this snatch of dialogue (playing both sides to me as his delighted audience):

> Are you all right? Need a glass of water?
> What? Don't worry about a glass of water right now.
> Watch your back, your posture is bad. That's going to hurt you some day.
> If I'm being shot at, that's going to hurt me.
> Sit up straight.
> No! My head will be out of the foxhole!
> Don't complain to me when your spine's hurting then.
> Please!
> You're grouchy, I'll get you a muffin.

Will spoke these lines out loud, but what he was doing was writing a sketch and by typing them up I've turned them into a script. Will gave another example of transposing behaviour which took us into considering *why* our character is behaving strangely. According to Will:

> People often walk into scenes at the UCB with a deliberately chosen, unusual philosophy that they picked as they were walking in. It might be something like, 'I'm going to be an army sergeant who loves yoga. I think that'll be unusual and funny.' That takes a little bit of planning, which is antithetical to a lot of people's improv instincts. You still don't know where it's going to go or what's going to happen but even by choosing that much, it's rebellious in the world of improv; or at least it was before UCB championed it.

In the case of the army sergeant who loves yoga, I'm thinking that the game could be that he's on the parade ground with a group of new recruits, drilling them, and he makes the kinds of sensitive, hands-on adjustments that a yoga teacher would make to poses. So, the sergeant major is behaving *as if* he is a yoga teacher.

Will went on, 'Often on stage your weird behaviour comes first, and then you have to figure out why you're doing it.' When encouraged to explain the reasons for their unusual behaviour, Will noted that, 'students would suddenly become much more specific in a good way. They would take this unusual behaviour and it would suddenly seem very human. Say *why* you're acting unusual and get grounded. Mike OT [actor and writer Michael Orton-Toliver] told me that when he taught at FA [the Free Association], he'd say, "I want you to justify yourself, not rationalize yourself." He was trying to communicate, "I want you to have a reason, but I don't want it to make a ton of sense."' It's an internal logic. It makes sense to the character, and we can understand why it makes sense to *them*, but from an objective standpoint it's absurd. 'But sometimes people would push too hard to say *why* and give themselves such full backstories and explanations that it ruined the scene.' It would be a level of detail more suited to the backstory of a sitcom or a film than an improv scene.

I was talking with Will online when my then ten-year-old daughter Kaia walked into the room. Will was pleased to meet her and Kaia told us she had just brought her guinea pigs in from their run in the garden. I told Will that I often like to joke about giving Kaia's guinea pigs inappropriate food such as sausages. When she left, inspired by her intervention, I turned again to the question of character motives and gave as an example a man in a sketch or an improv scene who wanted to feed sausages to a guinea pig. Typically, the reason why he wanted to do that would remain unexplained. It'd just be a crazy thing he did. However, seeking a justification for his behaviour, I suggested the character might want to kill off the guinea pig. Maybe he was fed up with having to clean its hutch out. (Not drawing on my own experience or anything.) However, Will offered a less extreme but still misguided motive: 'It could even just be as simple as them saying [to the guinea pig] "You need protein, you've got to have protein." The same sort of thing, in other words, that people say to each other when they're talking about diet. Or acting almost *as if* you're a worried mother: "He's wasting away in there. He looks like a skeleton. I'll drop in some pudding and a couple of sausages; just trying to toughen him up."' So, he *is* aware that it's outside the guinea pig's normal diet – and so needs some explaining – but the reason is not as outlandish as the one I proposed. And of course, for many of us this kind of parental or caregiver energy is very relatable and can be funny when pushed to a dysfunctional degree (shades of Mrs Doyle again here).

Returning to our sergeant major who behaves like a yoga teacher, in an improv context, you'd have to make bold, clear choices at the top of the scene to establish this, but marching on and ordering people around is in the nature of the character, so it feels doable in the right hands. But what if I walk in with this yoga sergeant major physicality and energy, but someone else gets in first and gives me a different role? According to Will, 'Even if you're [intending to be] a sergeant major, or you just have the energy of this confident, authoritarian type, then somebody labels you as the janitor or the low-status person in the group, you shouldn't change your personality. Just say yes to that. Yes, you are now in the low-status job but don't change your energy; that'll read as weird. Of course, it could end up being the fun part of the scene, that this person has this energy that doesn't fit their role.' It becomes a janitor behaving *as if* they are a sergeant major.

Developing characters for longer narratives

When you turn to a longer narrative, the demands on your characters change. Hollywood comedy guru Steve Kaplan said to me, 'You can do a sketch about a guy with an ass that's five times as big as anybody else's ass, and for two minutes, that can be hysterical, but can you watch that for a half-hour? Can you watch that for two hours? At some point, it's got to be about people and it's got to be about something that matters if it's going to be more than a few minutes.' As a rule of thumb, the more time the audience spends with a character, and so the more invested in them they are, the more developed they have to be. If our yoga-loving sergeant major is in an improv scene or a sketch, and they come and go, you probably don't need to worry too much about the implausibility of their behaviour, and any explanation needn't be that developed. But if it's a sitcom, the audience have to believe that they could somehow hold down this job drilling new army recruits and not get fired.

Moreover, sitcom might be called 'situation' comedy but in truth it's more about characters than situation. After her time at the BBC, Lucy Lumsden became head of comedy at Sky TV and amongst the more than sixty shows she commissioned was the supermarket sitcom *Trollied*. Lucy recalled, 'The workplace was what bound all our characters together, but in fact, the supermarket was often a very small component of that week's episode because what we were more interested in were the characters' personal stories. Because there's only so much you can do with a supermarket; spillages, lights going wrong, stocktake mistakes. And those things are not going to be the reason why you watch that show.'

Therefore, your characters need to be living, breathing beings in their own right, not just puppets fulfilling a function in your narrative. As Lucy Lumsden points out, 'You do see that a lot, in not-so successful comedies, where you get suspicious about characters and start to think, "This is just a construct." I'm speaking in very vague terms as I don't want to upset anyone, but there was a show recently with a group of performers, a gang really, very famous, and it should have worked but it was a tricky one.' The show was based on a real situation. 'So, they had plenty of stories, I don't think that was a problem. But I think early on they exhausted the point of each character. I wasn't curious to see what more there was to discover about each character. So, it was really reliant on comic set pieces really entertaining you in a sketchy way. You were delivered a diet of increasingly nightmarish situations they happened to be in. There was something lacking in depth about it and I suppose ultimately I didn't care because I didn't really buy them as three-dimensional characters in their own right.'

Lucy told me that an exercise she likes to do with writers is to identify a key attribute of the character you're creating and you then find people from your own life and experience who have that attribute and draw on them to develop the character. She said, 'For instance, if the character is an outsider who's awkward in social situations, it's just a simple exercise of asking yourself who in your life is like that?' Lucy went on to say you can choose five essential elements of the character that you then build up in this way, meaning you are creating a composite of a number of people. She concluded that 'the benefits of this is you've now got a real spine to your character. That's really, really helpful.' To give depth to characters beyond the situation we happen to meet them in, Lucy said another good exercise is to ask yourself:

> If this odd day wasn't happening, how would this character be spending their day? What would happen if they walked out of this scene; the scene you've created as a great playpen for them to show off how funny they are? They're going to walk out through that door and then what's going to happen? Where I find a lot of comic characters fall down, is that they've been created around a particular situation and I don't believe them beyond that. If that situation were to change, what's their purpose? It's hard work. Don't think it's easy. I think you have to spend days on characters. You don't just invent a character and assume everyone's going to buy it. You've got to lie brilliantly.

Another way to work towards a more rounded portrayal is to create a balance between positives and negatives as I describe in Chapter 1. To try this, firstly, think of someone in the public eye that you can't stand. Someone with power and influence who you find objectionable. Or ridiculous. Or laughable. A politician maybe. Or it could be an actor, a model, a singer. Now turn once again to page 5 for my table of positive and negative qualities and turn to the list of negatives. Pick three of them that fit this awful person you have chosen. It contains such gems as *egocentric*, *pretentious* and *touchy.* Enjoyable isn't it? Cathartic even. However, you now have to make a list of positive characteristics for this person you feel is objectionable. They don't think they are egocentric, pretentious and touchy, so if you just present them as this, then you are not presenting a real person. Now if you picked someone you really can't stand, this is not easy. It's a struggle. And yet you have to admit that they must have some good qualities. They've risen to this prominent position. They can't have done it solely on their negative qualities. So, pick their positives. Now you will have something like this: *dynamic, plucky, sincere/egocentric, pretentious, touchy.* And this is the beginning of a more rounded character. Now take this same approach with your objectionable fictional characters.

Here's another way of looking at your character from two perspectives: firstly, describe how they see themselves and secondly how others see them. If there is very little difference between these two perspectives then that would be a self-aware, functional person. The bigger the difference the more comic and/or tragic the character. Steve Coogan's appallingly brilliant Alan Partridge, for example, was based on a number of real-life British TV presenters. Many potential models for Partridge have been identified but (fortunately) there isn't one single person who embodies all of Partridge's traits, so it's very much an amalgamation of different individuals, and Coogan says there is a lot of himself in Partridge too. Here's how you might describe Alan Partridge in this way:

How Alan Partridge sees himself:
Charming, funny, relaxed, professional, friendly, popular
How others see him:
Petty, vindictive, neurotic, incompetent, loathsome, moribund

When you're developing a character, think in terms of the first list as how they see themselves when they're at their most self-regarding, and the second list as how others see them when they are most critical. This creates a persona and a shadow. List 1 is the persona they try to project, while list 2 is the shadow that undermines and contradicts the persona. This creates inner conflict. Comedy needs conflict between characters *and* conflict within characters. To explore this in action, try writing a scene where the character is trying to embody a quality or qualities from the first list while their efforts are undermined by qualities from the second list. In order for this to happen, think about a situation that will bring out their worst sides. As Lucy Lumsden said to me, 'Put your character in a situation where their greatest flaws are exposed.' You can also think of characters around them as 'trigger characters'. If your character, for instance, has an angry, impatient streak, then put them in a situation that requires tolerance and patience and pair them with a character who is slow and methodical. Your character will start off trying to be their best, but pretty soon their shadow will be triggered.

Steve Kaplan told me, 'In my new book *The Comic Hero's Journey*, I talk about the fact that in a longer form you have to put in real stakes, real loss, real feeling and real emotion. You can't be faking. If it's fake-y, then you're only as good as your last joke. Nobody's joke is that good. That's why a movie like *Scary Movie 4* is so terrible. Maybe a third of the jokes work, but that means that two-thirds of the jokes don't work and it's excruciating to sit through. But something like *Groundhog Day*, something like *Bridesmaids*, something like *40-Year-Old Virgin*, there's real emotion, pain and loss at the heart of each of those stories.' Success in comedy then is about much more than jokes. How did these films come to have heart and truth? The makers didn't simply make things up. They drew on the truth of their own lives and experiences and those of people around them. Judd Apatow, director of *Bridesmaids* and *The 40-Year-Old Virgin*, seeks a truthful starting point to anchor his bawdy stories. Apatow drew on his own insecurities for *40-Year-Old Virgin*, and the writers of *Bridesmaids*, Kristen Wiig and Annie Mumolo, drew on their experiences of being bridesmaids in order to present a truer, grittier picture of being a bridesmaid than the more familiar romanticized movie version. They wanted to reflect, as Wiig says, that being a bridesmaid can be 'a pain in the ass'.[4]

These two movies are based in recognizable, everyday worlds, but the other film Steve mentions, *Groundhog Day*, could scarcely be more fanciful in that a character gets stuck in a single day that repeats endlessly. However, what makes it such an enduring and beloved film is that it too is grounded in real emotion and truth. Steve Kaplan gave an example of this in a scene from the movie: 'Bill Murray told Harold Ramis about his own wedding day when after a long day, while his wife was sleeping, Bill poured his heart out to her. Harold Ramis took that and put that in the movie. That's the great scene when Andie MacDowell's sleeping and he's reading her a poem. He says that heartfelt thing, "I don't deserve someone like you but if ever I could be with you, I'd do whatever I could to make you happy." It's such a sweet moment and it doesn't come from an invention; it comes from life.'

In these first two chapters we have explored how your own life experience combined with close observation and exaggeration of others – from people intimately close to you, to work colleagues, to random strangers – can fuel your writing and performing. In the final chapter of this opening section, we look at how your interests, expertise and passions can inspire comedy.

---

[4] J. Winning, 'The Story Behind Bridesmaids', 2011, https://www.gamesradar.com/the-story-behind-bridesmaids/.

Chapter 3

Write What You Know and Love (or Hate)

Comedy, as much as any other form, can really benefit from specialist or inside knowledge. You might draw on a world you know well simply because it's a fertile context for comedy. Your intent could be purely whimsical, playing fast and loose with the reality, or it might be that you want the world to feel authentic and you're aiming for laughs of recognition. You might also have opinions and views you want to express, and you could even have a didactic intention where you hope the audience will learn from your piece.

Whatever your intent, the one piece of writing advice everyone has heard is 'write what you know'. Put simply, if you're writing about doctors then you'd better be a doctor; or at least, if you haven't actually gone to the trouble of becoming a doctor, then you need to do your research. Jed Mercurio famously drew on his background as a medic for his hit TV medical dramas; but because medical practice had moved on so much since his time in the 1990s, even he had to do his research. Then there are all the comedy practitioners from Dr Jonathan Miller to Harry Hill, Paul Sinha and Ken Jeong who actually were doctors and who, to a lesser or greater degree, draw on that knowledge in their creative life. Similarly, Jo Brand's time as a psychiatric nurse fuelled her nursing sitcom *Getting On* and for Chris Morris having GP parents led to a brace of disturbing doctor sketches in *Blue Jam* (and, later, *Jam*).

Monty Python's Graham Chapman, having abandoned his medical career for comedy, was able to draw on his knowledge for the, pre-*Python, Doctor in the House* sitcom scripts he wrote with John Cleese. This balance in a writing team of someone with professional or specialist knowledge and someone without, can be highly functional; you have the inside and the outside perspective. Improviser Katy Schutte told me that her friend Mark is a doctor, so I asked: what if he were improvising a scene as a doctor with another improviser playing a medic, but while *he* knows the facts and the terminology, his scene partner doesn't? Katy responded, 'If Mark were playing a doctor with someone who is speaking with the same amount of authority but with all the wrong words, then Mark has to use *their* terminology and they have to use Mark's terminology. It's a Venn diagram and the middle of it is where they ascend on. Somewhere in the middle, just a bit off, is hilarious. I think that's funnier than it being right or wrong.'

Memorably, the final episode of the *Monty Python* TV series included the 'Patient Abuse' sketch, notable for being co-written by non-Python Douglas Adams, in which Terry Jones as the patient rushes into the surgery clutching a stomach wound pouring blood. The disinterested doctor asks what happened and the patient cries out, 'I've just been stabbed by your nurse!' This leads to the patient having to complete 'the paperwork' before he can be seen, which is complicated by him needing to stem the blood; an indignity that is compounded by the questions on the form being a general knowledge trivia quiz. That particularly visceral *Python* sketch didn't really need a doctor's inside knowledge to co-write it. How much authentic knowledge you need, and how much accuracy the audience demand of you, is partly dependent on the style and form of comedy you are doing, a topic I go on to explore further in the next chapter, and also on your motivation for playing with the world in comedy.

I've called this chapter 'Write What You Know and Love (or Hate)' because knowing about a topic *and* having a strong opinion about it – positive or negative (and possibly both!) – is a great motivator to write. Rufus Jones' terrific show *Home*, about a Syrian refugee's experience of coming to the UK, was conceived when the refugee crisis in Europe was at its height. Jones was motivated by a sense of injustice and wanted to show the reality beyond the tabloid headlines. Youssef Kerkour plays Sami in the show and he told *British Comedy Guide* of his character: 'I always tell people, "Just think of Paddington, but instead of a cuddly bear, it's a big cuddly Syrian refugee."' He goes on, 'It's a story of a refugee who sneaks into the back of a car belonging to a lovely middle-class family on their way home from France. They get more than they bargain for when they arrive back home, and hilarity ensues. They help this refugee named Sami get back on his feet. The presence of this fourth person in the family starts to tug at the very nature of who they are, and their idea of home. Sami is a teacher, one of the middle class in Syria, who had to eventually leave during the war. His story mirrors that of many people coming out of Syria, one of whom is Hassan Akkad, who Rufus spoke to extensively throughout the writing process, and who was on set as an advisor.'

Akkad, who won a BAFTA for the extraordinary documentary film *Exodus*, like Sami had fled his home and job as an English teacher in Damascus. His role was to ensure the details of the asylum process were as realistic as possible and later he stepped into the role of dialectic coach, helping Kerkour with his Damascus accent.

In comedy, people often talk about 'punching up' as opposed to 'punching down'. Punching up is taking on those more powerful than you, and in the case of *Home* a major target of the comedy is the absurdities of the bureaucracy people like Sami have to face. Akkad says, 'I don't think any sane person could laugh at someone whose house has been destroyed, has had to do the journey and has been separated from his wife and child. We're being entertained by the reality that any refugee goes through once they arrive here.' Then there are the culture clash laughs and the family comedy, and Rufus Jones also sends up his own character, Peter, who is wont to spout noxious opinions about refugees, views that are challenged by the arrival of Sami. Jones observes, 'He probably doesn't necessarily believe half of what he's saying, but he's full of received wisdom. And it's really a reflection from his own inadequacies.'

When you have dark, challenging or dramatic material, one device that helps keep the comedy to the fore is to undercut the seriousness. This is *bathos.* For example, in a potentially dry sequence in *Home* where Sami learns about the reality of the asylum bureaucracy from a Home Office civil servant, it's given a lift by taking place over an impromptu pint in a pub. It's also undercut by some comic business with wasabi peas – a novel and perplexing snack to Sami. In a later set-piece scene, in his despair Sami has taken someone hostage and the police have been called. Levity and bathos are lent to the situation due to it playing out in a rather chi-chi spa. You can imagine Jed Mercurio writing the equivalent hostage scene in a police drama – but he'd be unlikely to set it in a spa where the police officer is keeping the operation low key 'out of respect for the energy of the space'![1]

Research in stand-up comedy

A stand-up who does a lot of reading and research to inspire his comedy is Daniel Audritt. I directed Daniel's 2019 stand-up show *Better Man*, which was about masculinity and was seen at the Edinburgh Fringe and Soho Theatre. The jokes and routines around masculinity were all drawn from research and moulded into material. Daniel told me, 'For the show, I did a lot of research on love, about opposites attracting and also about breaking down myths of romcoms. Studying like that you just hope that you can pull out the funny ideas at a later date. The dream situation is when you have the reading, the thought process and then you hit on a funny angle. A lot of the time I do lots of reading and it'll go around my head for ages, but I can't find the funny way into it. And sometimes you read about thirty pages and it ends up being just two jokes; but still that's good enough.' The next step towards turning fascinating facts into comedy is to make

---

[1] 'Home interviews', *British Comedy Guide*, n.d., https://www.comedy.co.uk/tv/home/interview/.

it personal. Daniel explains, 'I'll read something and I'll think, "Oh, that's interesting, how does that relate to my life?" For example, I was reading a lot about the differences between men and women when it comes to parenthood. That made me think, even though I'm not a parent, as a guy I really like babies. I think they're very cute. Then I started thinking about language and the kind of words women say about kids and how it could sound creepy if you transposed them to men.' Daniel went through examples, such as 'Oh that baby is so cute, I'd like to take it home, I'd like to eat it . . .', which coming from a playful female sounds fine, but from a man, less so. As he worked on the routine, he recalled, 'When you've got an idea in your head and your mind is open to it, you start overhearing things. I remember hearing a woman seeing a cute baby and saying, "My ovaries are going to explode." If the equivalent came from a man it'd sound horrible and creepy: "My testicles are going to explode!" That became the payoff to the piece. That shows the disconnect between how men and women can talk about kids.'

Having made it personal, the next step is to put it into a context and into a narrative. Alongside his stand-up, Daniel writes sketch and sitcom scripts with Kat Butterworth (see Chapter 7). He told me, 'Kat also supports my stand-up. When I have an observation, she'll always say, "Put it in a story." So, it still has the nuts and bolts of an observational comedy routine but slipped into a life story. The narrative element helps the buy-in. It's a question of how do I do all of this in a way that feels like I'm just talking. So, I say "I was invited to a baby shower." Truth is, I've never been to a baby shower. It was just the best way of telling a story that allows me to get in all of that research, in a way that felt like I was just living my life and it was accessible.'

Daniel discovered in his background reading for *Better Man* that people often believe arguing with your partner shows you care. This became a routine, and when I went to see the show during its run at Soho Theatre, to get into the topic, Daniel asked a couple if they feel it's romantic to argue. Simultaneously the man said 'Yes' and the woman said 'No'. When Daniel pointed out what had just happened it got a huge reaction from the audience and I wondered what the chances are of that happening on any given night. Daniel told me, 'That was such a nice moment, and you'd be surprised how often that happens. It was maybe the tenth time including the Edinburgh run. Chances are, every show, there was a couple in the room I could ask that to and they'd give me that response. It's just a case of whether or not I found them!'

Comedians will often have stock types in mind that they are looking for in the audience in order to peg material to. In Daniel's case:

I'm usually looking for four types. A new couple, an older couple, a guy who I feel like I can talk to about masculinity, and a girl in her twenties who I can talk to about her experience of men's behaviour. In the first 15 minutes, while I'm doing jokes, I'm reading the room, trying to see who to talk to. It has to be in the front row or two because if it looks like you're searching too hard for them it ruins the belief in the spontaneity. I'm asking, 'What's going to be the most fruitful place for me to fish?' I'm using the conversation with them to get into jokes. That's all I'm trying to do, but it'll make you feel like I'm in the room. It's a little bit like improv. It's fairly easy to gauge a new couple just based on body language alone, like the guy's got his hand on her knee. A newish couple would tend to do that. For this show, I'm always looking for a certain kind of man to talk to. At the Soho Theatre show you saw, there was the very put together, handsome black guy on the front row. He was perfect. He was also the person in a new relationship and he served to be my touchstone for the kind of new masculinity I want to talk about. If you go to a guy and say, 'You look pretty put together. Are you using men's beauty products?' and they go 'No', it makes your observation feel less true. So, I have to be a bit careful over who I'm going for. It does still happen, but I've got better at reading someone and thinking, 'He'll say no.' Also, it's fine if you have someone who doesn't use them but they're open to it. That won't stop you in your tracks.

In the end the material has moved so far from the research that inspired it, you wouldn't realize the origins. Daniel says, 'Nobody knows I've read a single book! There's two ways of doing it. You can be a comic like Ahir Shah whose work I love. They are very upfront with their intelligence and their reading. They'll say, "I've done this research" and it works. But with my persona, I can't do that. I don't think the audience want it from me. I'm too much of a friend of the audience [as opposed to high-status]. Also, I feel like a bit of a dickhead doing it! Standing in front of a group people being like, "I've done all this reading" – I want to relate to the audience, not teach the audience.'

UK-based American comedian Robyn Perkins, on the other hand, openly acknowledges the reading and research behind her shows. Robyn got started in comedy on my London stand-up course and is now a professional comic. She has a strong science background and over time it's come increasingly into her comedy. She told me, 'I was a marine biologist which is very research driven. I realized that when I go to write anything, the first thing I do is research. That's how I was trained. So, I decided to embrace that in the comedy I was writing. I think a lot of comics will come up with a premise and write jokes, whereas I will come up with a premise, research it and then find jokes out of the research.' Again, the next step is to make it personal, and for Robyn a lot of her comedy comes from applying something very technical or scientific to her own life: 'It is funny in and of itself, the absurdity that I go through to analyse my life. There is just funniness in the fact that I literally have a quadratic equation explaining how long you should take before you text somebody back. Every aspect of my life, I overanalyse, and so it seems natural to take that aspect of my character and blow it up to the extreme.'

Robyn also hopes the audience will learn something at her shows, as does Australian stand-up mathematician Matt Parker. Another graduate of my stand-up course, I've worked with Matt over a number of years, including working on early *Festival of the Spoken Nerd* shows, and most recently directing his *Humble Pi* tour, based on his bestselling book of the same name (*Humble Pi: A Comedy of Maths Errors*, alternatively subtitled *When Math Goes Wrong in the Real World* in the States). While Matt does performances with a clear teaching agenda, like his support slot on the Royal Institution Christmas Lectures with Hannah Fry, I put it to him that even when he's doing comedy shows he still has an educational intent. He responded, 'Yes, even when it's advertised and sold as a comedy show, I want the audience to go away having seen actual maths and why it's useful, and what you can do with it. Even when it's *not* useful; why it's interesting, why it's engaging. People get too hung up on remembering a thing you've learned. Even if they don't remember any of it when they leave, at least at the time they were following along. All scientists and mathematicians, you learn a thing, then you forget that thing. But you know you can look it up again.'

If you're going down this fact-based route, how do you avoid it being a lecture with jokes? Not that there's anything wrong with a lecture with jokes, but when you're selling a comedy show it needs to be more than that. The answer again is to make it personal and put it in a context; to create a narrative around the facts. Matt says, 'I'm a big fan of John Oliver's *Last Week Tonight* where he does these long-form bits where it'll be quite a serious topic and then suddenly, there'll just be this random joke . . . and then you're back into the content.' These are jokes to sweeten the pill of the serious content:

When my first draft of my books go in, I'll literally get it back from my editor with 'joke here' notes. Basically, it's been too long since there was a treat for the reader, and so I've got to write a joke and put it in there. When I watch John Oliver, I can almost see these notes written on the original script. 'Joke here. Joke here'. It works, but I'm way happier when the content you're trying to get across feeds the jokes. For example, I've got a routine on binary codes; converting text into ones and zeros. And I've got a scarf my mum made for me, and it's covered in binary codes. I turn it into a story about how she had to talk to my brother, who's also a nerd, to find out how to do the binary in the first place. Then I talk about my relationship with my brother and how we email in binary code, and all these weird things. On one hand, it's funny because it's the story of the family interacting and a mum trying to please her nerdy kids, and her obsession with knitting and my obsession with maths. But what I love about it is the really funny bits are her discovering she made a mistake in the scarf, and then me pointing out the implications of that mistake.

The jokes here are about the way binary codes work and the way error correction works, and it wouldn't have been funny if it wasn't for the fact that the audience had learned earlier about error correction and binary codes. That's very satisfying. This is the thing that distinguishes between a lecture tarted up with jokes and a proper show.

Show not tell

Another familiar piece of writing advice is to 'show, not tell', and as anyone doing a science or factual talk who has ever done a demonstration knows, it's more powerful if people can see it happening. In Robyn Perkins' *10,000 Decisions* stand-up show, she draws on anecdotes, family stories and neuroscience to talk about decision-making. I asked her how the show came about and she explained, 'I decided to embrace the idea of using science to explain the issues I have in my life. I'm very indecisive, so why is this? To find out, I started researching. I read a lot of books and found out the top neuroscientist in decision-making happened to be in London and so we grabbed a coffee and basically I asked her all the questions I had.' Rather than simply *talking* through all the material she'd discovered (with added jokes), in each show a well thought-out decision is actually made for an anonymous audience member! As Robyn elaborated, 'Every show, I would get my audience members to anonymously submit a decision that they're struggling with, and I would pick one. Then we'd go through the way that your brain makes decisions, and together as an audience we'd make the decision.' So the subject of the show is actually happening as part of it.

One of the central topics in Matt Parker's *Humble Pi* book is how computer clocks that keep time by counting down can cause the whole system to crash when they reach zero. Alarmingly this can happen in aircraft. (We learn that the solution, as with all IT problems, is to periodically turn the plane off and on again.) To mimic this real-world problem, in the book the page numbers count down and they crash when they hit zero! Matt says, 'I thought it was very funny. It took a lot of time to convince my publisher to do it, but they did.' We felt it'd be great if the show itself had the same problem. To make this happen, we introduced a countdown timer (justified as helping Matt avoid running over his timeslot) which when it hit zero unexpectedly causes the whole show to break down: the sound system fails, the lights go down, the AV goes haywire. Matt remarks, 'Yes, that was fun because I ended up making the show overly complicated, with programming and lasers and automated bits, then I spend the whole show fighting against a system of my own creation, that eventually lets me down. It's pretty funny. What's very satisfying is, for the audience they've heard stories in the show where counting down causes things to crash, and they've seen I'm keeping track of time in the show by counting down, but it doesn't seem to occur to them that it will happen to the show. So, when it does, everyone was like, "He totally warned this is what goes wrong with this kind of system!"'

Absurd and disproportionate effort

If you are doing comedy shows that draw on your real-life passions, another route to finding the funny is to ramp up any obsessional side you might have. Matt Parker is also the host of *An Evening of Unnecessary Detail* at the Back Yard Comedy Club in London, where you can see comedians who have an obsession or some arcane knowledge they want to share alongside scientists and academics with a comedic touch. Matt observes, 'I think a lot of comedians are closet nerds. To become a comedian, you've got to be a certain amount of obsessive anyway, to analyse why things do or don't work, and obsession and passion are entertaining to watch.' And a natural way it starts to become funny, is when that passion is disproportionate or misplaced:

> It gets funnier the more out of step their passion is, and the more effort they've gone to and the deeper their obsession goes. Actually, that's one of the best ways to do a topic other people may not care about: go further than any reasonable human should. That is, in my opinion, innately hilarious. It doesn't matter how boring the content is, if you've just gone one step too far with your obsession, with logging train stations in a spreadsheet, or visiting locations from a film or anything that otherwise could be quite boring, that's hilarious.

In *Humble Pi*, Matt takes apart a series of TV advertisements that have faulty mathematics, for example in McDonald's and Pepsi commercials: 'In an advert, McDonald's miscalculated how many meal combinations there are from their fast food menu.' As we worked on the show, I asked Matt, 'What was happening in that meeting when the advertisers were trying to write the ad?' (This is following my 'What before?' question, or 'How did this come about?' See chapter 2 in my first book, *A Director's Guide to the Art of Stand-up*.) Matt ran with this and created an act out: 'There's three distinct characters in that meeting. They've all got the same voice. I just stand in slightly different places on stage. It's very different from the book and really works on stage. It wouldn't work in a book.' While you could write it as dialogue in a book, what you'd be missing is Matt's attitude towards these people as he portrays them: 'I'm playing the characters semi-sarcastically. I'll roll my eyes at the audience. It's all very funny, because my disdain for their slapdash approach to maths is coming through.' Furthermore, a big part of the funniness is that Matt *really* cares that the maths was wrong in the advert: 'That's what I discovered when I was on the circuit, in comedy clubs. I wasn't doing maths content then but I was still very nerdy, and the comedy was in the fact that reality didn't match my nerdy expectations; I expect the world to be nice and logical, and I'm almost unaware of how out of step with other people I am. I'll be like, "Why do they do it that way when *this* is the logical way to do it. I don't understand."' By the end of the *Humble Pi* show, Matt reveals that he has actually *remade* those old adverts with the mathematics corrected! 'I spent way more money on this, and time, and effort than I should have. I hired a studio with a green screen, we filmed in locations all over the place to try and recreate the shots from this old Pepsi commercial. We did 3D modelling. Maybe in hindsight, I wasted a lot of money! But that's the point. It's this ridiculous thing to do.'

Matt's remaking of the adverts was indeed completely ridiculous and, on the other hand, very impressive. I find this a pleasing area for comedy to operate in – that interface between the daft and the deeply committed; for example, Dave Gorman's breakthrough show *Are You Dave Gorman?*, where he set out to track down and meet his namesakes all over the world. Matt admits, 'I do enjoy comedy that is project-oriented. It's got all the narrative things you need. You start off with a quest, there's adversity along the way, then you end up with the thing. I find that funny and hugely satisfying.' Helen Wood is a writer and performer for whom I have directed three shows about her obsessions. The success of the second show, about Helen's love of (paper) Ordnance Survey maps, *The OS Map Fan Club*, and its appeal to an enthusiastic niche older audience meant the follow-up show, *The National Trust Fan Club*, was picked up by producer James Seabright for a run at the Gilded Balloon at the Edinburgh Fringe and a national tour. One problem when we began the show was it didn't have the same nerdy passion as is aroused by OS Maps. The answer was to make it a quest. What could that quest be? To visit every one of the 500+ National Trust places. (Spoiler: in the show she hasn't got there yet, but the madness and obsessiveness of the quest brings a lot of comedy to proceedings.) Having done three shows about her obsessions, Helen says, 'The perfect situation is when you have someone on stage who is passionate about a topic and the audience are too.'

Richard Lindesay, the offbeat comedian who started out as a one-liner comic, has recently pivoted to a musical act that is built on this comic friction between something that is very impressive and, at the same time, absurd. I have worked with New Zealander Richard over several years and it was my suggestion to him that he find a strong 'set-piece' to close his act, something that was funny *and* impressive, that ultimately led to this new musical direction. When we spoke, Richard recalled, 'I first tried to find that with verbal jokes and then I tried a couple of prop things, which were quite clever but not impressive enough and I was struggling. I was grasping at straws, thinking, "What else can I do?" Then it just came to me, "Well I can play the flute, but of course you couldn't use that." Then I thought, "Hang on, or can you?"'

Once he'd had this epiphany, Richard and I worked together on finding comic angles for the flute. One of our first thoughts was have a spoken set-up and then something played on the flute would be the payoff. Richard's experience writing one-liners meant his mind was primed for this kind of thinking. To get the ball rolling I asked, 'What is the flute useful for?' One of Richard's answers was 'It's good for if you're in a situation where you need to disguise a fart.' Richard describes the gag this became: 'I'm playing something quite beautiful and then I'm obviously getting a bit tense and then at the moment of release I do an octave jump. That's where it started.' What began as a search for a set-piece ended up transforming Richard's act from an offbeat one-liner style to a truly novel and eccentric musical act. 'It wasn't long before everything I was doing with the flute was becoming a bit of a set-piece! It slowly took over what I did.' Richard went on:

> Often people advise, 'Do something to encourage a cheer when you come on stage.' So what I'll do is I'll wave a flute up, and then they cheer. Then I switch it to like I'm conducting their cheers with the flute. I put the flute up higher for more cheers and bring it down slowly and then move the cheer around the room. Pointing to different people and then pointing at specific people and them cheering as I point the flute to them. It's become very interactive like that, which doesn't require a word. Another example is I have the recorder and I have a conducting baton. I say that a useful thing about the recorder is it's good for setting up an impromptu orchestra. Then I set up different parts [for] the audience to do rhythmic clapping or whacking their knees to make the 'We Will Rock You' stomping. Then I have a designated singer who, at the point where the singing comes in, I point to. And they either sing or they don't. Either way is funny. The climax is me playing the song's guitar solo on the recorder. It goes down very, very well.

Richard also stumbled upon a physical clowning dimension. 'It was almost by accident. At one gig, I took the [folded up] flute stand out of my pocket and people didn't know what it was.' Richard started to unfold it and, aware of their sudden interest, he took his time and made it theatrical. 'Then when I'd put it together, I put it down on the stage, put the flute on it and they applauded! It got me into more of a clowning approach, which is paying attention to the reaction of the audience and going with what they're enjoying. I found it was usually when I made a mistake that they found it funny. Then I'd embellish on the mistake. If I'm trying something complex with multiple instruments and I drop one, they always laugh. So, I was like, "Right I'll drop one at that point every time."'

It was when Richard began to bring in multiple instruments that he went into the area of very impressive/completely ludicrous that can yield such comedy: 'I've got various pieces where I'll use multiple instruments. For instance, there's a piece where I set up the premise that a problem with being a flute player is you don't have friends, and if you don't have friends it's hard to do duets. Therefore, you've got to make do and do it by yourself.' And so Richard plays the flute and the recorder simultaneously. We worked on this backstory together, which turns what would have just been a spectacle into a narrative:

> Because you've only got one hand for each, this meant only using the notes you can play with one hand on these instruments. I start playing the flute with one hand and then I try to play the recorder as well. I'll be failing to do that and looking puzzled, adding a bit of 'clowniness' to it. Then I finally realize I can play the flute with one hand and have the recorder in my nose and then play them both at the same time. Then I harmonize with them both. I guess the impressiveness there is that I've bothered harmonizing too. As well as doing playing two instruments I actually am accompanying myself. Me struggling to get it and *then* getting it is funnier than me just being able to go and do it. It builds up the energy and suspense. 'Is he going to be able to do it?' Probably in the back of their minds they know I can or else I wouldn't be starting, but there's a moment of suspending disbelief. They enjoy me not being able to do it.

From looking for a skill to make a set-piece, Richard has discovered a whole new act which has also reignited his love for music. He says, 'The comedy has got me back into playing the flute. I've been getting professional lessons and I've been learning to play better than I ever could. Really trying to make it so that if orchestral fluters come along that they would be happy with how I'm playing.' That *is a* word by the way, 'fluters'. Comedy audiences are certainly happy with Richard's act, and at the time of writing Richard is in the final of the Musical Comedy Awards at Bloomsbury Theatre in London. A very unexpected development for the deadpan one-liner comic I first worked with and whom I wrote about in my first book.

When you're talking about or doing something you love, it's immediately engaging for an audience. Witness the success of the Boring Conference where 'interesting people talk about boring things'. What makes it work is each speaker's enthusiasm for their ostensibly tedious topic. What interest or obsession do you have in your life that you're not currently channelling into your comedy? If it's not obviously exciting, even better. Your zeal for your subject will be a big part of the funniness. Furthermore, while research can feel like a chore to a writer who is happier making stuff up, researching a topic you are fascinated by is a pleasure, and your passions and enthusiasms are naturally inspiring to write about. Returning to TV comedy, Graham Chapman's mountaineering interest led to an unusual number of sketches about mountaineers in *Monty Python*, including the one where the double-vision sufferer Sir George Head,

OBE (a relative of mine?) is recruiting climbers for an assault on the 'twin peaks' of Mount Kilimanjaro.

In this opening section we have explored how your life, observations, knowledge and enthusiasms are all grist for your comedy mill. In the next section we turn to crafting comedy action.

PART TWO

Action

Chapter 4
Games and Worlds

When I originally started teaching comedy (many, many years ago) I would talk about focusing on 'the central comic idea' of the scene. Then when I was introduced to the work of the Upright Citizens Brigade Theatre (UCB), I immediately saw how their thinking dovetailed with my own and, what's more, I quickly picked up this very useful term: the *game* of a scene (the one word 'game' replacing my original four). Many times in this chapter, and throughout the book, I use this word 'game' but in the improv world, there are varying notions as to what constitutes a 'game' as well as dissenting voices who question the value of looking at a scene as having a 'game' at all. However, for comedy scenes where you want a clear, focused idea it's a very helpful perspective, both in improv itself and in scripted comedy.

My introduction to the concept of the 'game' of a scene began an ongoing and fruitful engagement with improv and so I was delighted to speak with UCB teacher and author Will Hines, who we met in Chapter 2. Will told me, 'The Upright Citizens Brigade Theatre, where I've trained and where I teach, even though it is improv, is very writerly in its approach. I'm simplifying greatly, but the group who founded the theatre tried to make improv feel more like a sketch. Just having one unusual thing, not multiple unusual things, having a voice-of-reason. They came from a disorganized, chaotic scene and they liked it very clean and organized, and so that results in an improv theatre that becomes much more idea-based. I've always thought that the founders [Matt Besser, Ian Roberts, Matt Walsh, Amy Poehler] put a priority on making a comedic point and getting there quickly.' In UCB thinking, if you enter an improv scene looking for the game, the 'unusual thing' in the situation, the scene will more naturally have a comedic focus. I first learned the word 'game' at UCB, who champion it. The founders studied with Del Close in Chicago in the 1990s. Del was directing them and came up with the word 'game' but then the UCB really ran with it, and then when they moved to New York and set up a school, they really doubled down on that idea. They like having one game per scene. You could have a sub-game or a character game but know what your main one is.'

Games, sub-games and character games are useful concepts both for managing ideas emerging on the fly in improvisation and for scripting scenes with a clear comedic dynamic and hierarchy of ideas. Comedy Central sketch duo Key & Peele, who began in improv, aim to have multiple layers to a sketch. Keegan-Michael Key says that they always try to make sure their sketches have three levels. For instance, there'll be the comedic game, the look of the piece and perhaps there will be a touch of homage or parody. He cites as an example the job interview sketch from season 5. Drawing on their improv background, this sketch was one where they did a very large amount of improvising on the day of filming, resulting in a very different sketch from the original script. The game of the scene is an interviewee (Peele) waiting to go into a job interview and having to listen to the previous applicant getting into a passionate bromance with the interviewer (Key), with them both laughing and joking uproariously, rendering the rest of the interviews a formality. Then there's the sub-game of setting the scene in the 1970s, which Key describes as 'unnecessary' to the main premise, and thirdly there is the character game of the interviewer constantly playing pranks.[1]

Another example of this kind of layering is found in *Fleabag*. In an interview with *Deadline*, Phoebe Waller-Bridge explained that when writing scenes, she likes to have at least three things going on. For example, in the scene where Fleabag is trying to impress the bank manager as she applies for a business loan, firstly she is underprepared, which is the main business of the scene. This basic premise is then given a second layer by Fleabag being hot and sweaty, and furthermore she has forgotten to put a top on underneath her jumper. Eventually she is so hot, she tries to take off her jumper, and accidentally flashes the bank manager. What's more, the situation is further complicated by the bank manager, played by Hugh Dennis, being in the middle of a sexual harassment scandal which has devastated him and caused him to separate from his wife. In the terms we're discussing, you've got the main game of the scene (try to impress the manager despite being underprepared), a sub-game (being hot and sweaty) and a character game (the bank manager devastated at the harassment scandal). Waller-Bridge says that when there are three things going on at the same time, at a minimum, you instantly have reality.[2]

---

[1] J. D. Fox, 'Keegan-Michael Key's 11 Favorite Sketches From Key & Peele's Final Season', *Vulture*, 26 August 2016, https://www.vulture.com/2016/08/key-peele-favorite-season-five-sketches.html.
[2] A. Blyth, 'Phoebe Waller-Bridge On Bringing Bond Into The Present, Why Femaleness Can't Be Categorized & The New Project That Came To Her In A Dream', *Deadline*, 5 June 2019, https://deadline.com/2019/06/phoebe-waller-bridge-bond-25-eclipse-fleabag-killing-eve-emmys-1202626221/.

Games, sub-games and character games (in *Monty Python* sketches at the British Library)

One of my most enjoyable teaching gigs is running a weekend comedy writing workshop at the British Library in London, not least because the weekend course begins with a show-and-tell from a curator of the library's archive where we have an exclusive, up-close-and-personal viewing of original, often handwritten, *Monty Python* scripts from the Michael Palin archive. As we look at these artefacts, I take the opportunity to talk about the concepts of games, sub-games and character games as they play out in classic *Python* sketches whilst beginning to introduce the language and perspectives I'll be using as we develop and write our own scenes and sketches.

On the most recent weekend course, curator Greg Buzwell explained to us, 'This is my favourite archive in the Library. It's actually quite a new one. Michael donated it to us, which is incredibly generous when you think what it could have achieved on the open market. The part we've got covers his career from his very early days up to the late 1980s. It includes all of the *Monty Python* material.' Picture the scene. We are in a stylish seminar room in the British Library in London and on a table before us are laid out fifty-year-old notebooks with comedy history inside. Literally within touching distance. (But probably best we don't touch.) Greg shows us a volume of Palin's diaries and says:

> Michael kept a diary pretty much since *Python* began. This is just one of literally hundreds of volumes. It's pretty much daily. There's a reference here to performing 'Pet Shop Parrot' [as it was known at that point] on 20 June 1970. I think it's the first time it was actually performed for an audience. It was performed at a fundraising event, called 'Oh Hampstead'. The programme wasn't in the archive when it arrived, but we did a little display of the diaries and this page of the diary was on display. Someone who saw the exhibition came in and says, 'I've got the programme if you want it.' That's quite a rare survival. The other sketch they performed was about a Minister whose legs fall off, which was done by John Cleese and Graham Chapman.

Did that sketch ever see the light of day again? Greg goes on, 'They were obviously trying out new material for this particular audience at a fundraiser.'

Greg then turns the pages of a notebook of Palin's handwritten *Python* scripts and explains, 'Most of it is Michael's handwriting, but every so often Terry Jones's handwriting appears. They're obviously using the same notebook, almost certainly sitting side by side, and bouncing ideas between the pair of them.' Greg turns to an example: 'Here's the Spam Sketch, which is in Michael Palin's handwriting. Of course, the phrase "spam email" comes from this sketch.' In the sketch, a couple are ordering food in a greasy spoon cafe where all the dishes have spam in them. Here is an excerpt from the menu: 'egg and spam; egg, bacon and spam; egg, bacon, sausage and spam; spam, bacon, sausage and spam; spam, egg, spam, spam, bacon and spam . . .' The *game* of the sketch is trying to order a dish without spam in a cafe that serves nothing but wildly spam-infused dishes. The rhythm of the list is carefully played, and having the benefit of the written text to study we can see that there are many small rewrites and adjustments to the menu items to improve the rhythm. There was a lot of rewriting evident in the scripts. For example, squinting closely at the original handwritten script, I saw a nice example of a rewritten line. In the original line, the woman, Mrs Barton, says 'Have you got anything without spam?' The waitress originally replies with something like (the handwriting was rather messy), 'Egg, bacon, and sausage. But it'll probably taste of spam.' This was crossed out and changed to 'Well, there's spam, eggs, sausage and spam. That's not got much spam in it,' which is a funnier line. When I read the original line out to the rest of the group at the British Library, it got a smile; then I read the rewritten line and it got a big laugh. Often the first version of the line gives you the idea, and then you can finesse it and make it funnier. You can imagine Palin and Jones playing around with variations of the line until they got one that made them laugh.

There are two *points of view* in the sketch: on one side you have the woman who doesn't like spam and wants a dish without it, and on the other her husband, the waitress and an incongruous group of Viking diners who are all on board with the idea of spam with everything. The waitress and all those who love spam have an *unreasonable point of view*. They simply can't get enough of the stuff and are not deviating from this path. Meanwhile, the customer is the *voice-of-reason* who would like some flexibility in the menu as she tries to manoeuvre around the immovable obstacle of the unreasonable waitress. Speculating about the origins of the Palin–Jones Spam sketch, I recalled that my daughter recently wanted pancakes and maple syrup for breakfast in a cafe and had to order 'pancakes, maple syrup and bacon – without the bacon'. I was immediately put in mind of the Spam sketch: perhaps it was itself inspired by a cafe that was inflexible with their menu items? Often comedy ideas have their basis in the absurdities of everyday life, and even the most outlandish concepts are best grounded in a recognizable dynamic from real life.

Greg then shows us another notebook. 'This is, again, one of Michael's notebooks. As you can see, it's very anarchic: lots of doodles. I think this was done when all the Pythons were sitting around the table in a meeting, and they're working on a running order for their sketches.' This was for the Spanish Inquisition episode of the *Flying Circus*, series 2, episode 2, first broadcast on 22 September 1970. Greg points to a scrawled list surrounded by doodles: 'I brought this one along because I think it's a great example of how anarchic, creative and freestyle a lot of their meetings must have been. You get strange squiggles and doodles. Some of the doodles we actually reproduced in the Palin archive exhibition graphics, and we had to go back to Michael to say "Is this one of your doodles, or is it Terry Jones's?" And of course, he can't remember. Why should he? It's fifty years ago, but he thought most of the doodles were probably his. Here, you can see the names of different sketches written down. You have the Spanish Inquisition. There's the Raymond Luxury Yacht interview. There's the Semaphore version of *Wuthering Heights*.'

For those who don't know them, I explain to the group that the Raymond Luxury Yacht sketch features an absurd man with no credentials (and an enormous fake nose) attempting to be interviewed on TV. As Steve Kaplan says, put your characters (your non-heroes) in situations where they don't have the requisite skills or knowledge but nevertheless they're trying to get what they want (in this case to be on TV). Secondly, the *game* of the *Wuthering Heights* sketch is that all the dialogue in a TV dramatization of the novel is conveyed through semaphore flags, and you have Heathcliff and Catherine communicating with each other across the moor using flags. Greg comments, 'That one makes me laugh, because when they're shouting it's much bigger flags, and you then have the baby in the pram with tiny little flags.' While the word '*game*' used in this way wasn't a term that had currency at the time the Pythons themselves were writing, looking back we can use it to describe what they were doing, and looking forward it will help us in our own future work. It becomes particularly helpful in more dense scenarios when we bring in the term's siblings: sub-games and character games.

The Spanish Inquisition, the third piece Greg references, is a multi-part series of sketches and has a complex layering of *games*, *sub-games* and *character games*. The *set-up* of the opening sketch in the sequence begins with what is evidently a drama in a northern mining town. There is theme music and a caption. Then the dialogue starts between a working-class northern mill worker (Graham Chapman) and a middle-class women (Carol Cleveland). There's trouble at the mill. The woman wants to know what kind of trouble. Chapman explains that 'one of the cross beams has gone out askew on the treadle' but the woman has no idea what he's talking about. He doesn't really know either and, feeling interrogated and getting defensive, the man says, 'I didn't expect a kind of Spanish Inquisition' (i.e. he didn't expect an interrogation). At which point there is a dramatic, jarring chord and three members of the Spanish Inquisition burst in (Palin, Jones and Terry Gilliam) and exclaim that 'No one expects the Spanish Inquisition!' A breathtaking leap.

For all of its anachronisms, not least the Spanish Inquisition being in the wrong historical era, the *game* at the heart of the sketch is the trio of inquisitors trying and failing to be a terrifying force who can extract confessions. These again are characters who lack the skills they need but nevertheless keep trying to get what they want despite their limitations. First of all, they fail to deliver an intimidating speech, despite multiple takes, where they have to keep going off and coming in again, with the now bored Graham Chapman having to repeatedly provide the cue line: 'I didn't expect a kind of Spanish Inquisition.' Latterly they have failed to bring the torture instrument, the rack, to use on Carol Cleveland, instead bringing a washing-up drying rack. There's a *sub-game* running through the scene in which the use of captions on TV is subverted; at the start a caption comes up telling us that it's 'Jarrow, New Year's Eve 1911', but with a title card featuring a modern nuclear power plant. And then bells ring midnight and the caption changes to 'Jarrow, 1912'. Later on, after a burst of evil laughter from the cardinals, an on-screen caption reads 'DIABOLICAL LAUGHTER', followed by a caption that in a moment of *meta-comedy* reads 'DIABOLOCAL ACTING'.

There's also a very random *character game* in this sketch – one of the inquisitors is Biggles, the flying ace from 1930s–1960s children's books. He wears a red cardinal's uniform topped off with a flying cap with goggles, and he has a British accent and a bristling moustache. Initially, Palin's Cardinal Ximénez gives up on the speech and attempts to get Cardinal Biggles to do it, who also fails. And later it is Biggles who has brought the washing-up rack by mistake and has to tie Carol Cleveland to it, and to Palin's embarrassment, goes through the motions of turning it to torture her. In the next sketch of the sequence, the game of being hopeless at torturing and extracting confessions continues when their method of torment is to seat an old lady in 'the comfy chair'. It was a hallmark of *Monty Python* to have this dense layering of detail, and it helps us keep track of it all by thinking in terms of *games*, *sub-games* and *character games*.

Meanwhile, back at the British Library, we come to the scripts for *Monty Python's Life of Brian* and we see the sketch where the *game* is Pontius Pilate not understanding joke Roman names. Greg explains, 'We had it displayed in a show in the Treasures Gallery. I think it's suitably surreal because the Treasures Gallery is, basically, all the top treasures, it's all illuminated manuscripts, and then in one corner, there was this one thing saying "Biggus Dickus". For the British Library, it was quite radical.' When we turn to the films, we are also seeing these individual sketches becoming scenes in a longer narrative; they become the *set-pieces* that the plot is constructed around. Greg turns to the Lazarus sketch in Palin's handwritten *Life of Brian* scripts. He asks 'Has anyone heard of the Lazarus sketch?' We haven't. He explains: 'It didn't make it into the film. I think Michael, in the diary, mentions that he thought it was a bit too "student revue", so he didn't use it'. The *game* of the sketch is that Lazarus, having been raised from the dead, goes to see his doctor. His doctor says "I didn't expect to see you again," and says he's thrown away all of his notes. Then he asks "What seems to be the problem?" And Lazarus says he thinks he's suffering from "post-death depression", and also fears that he's likely to die again, to which the doctor says

"Well, it's always on the cards, isn't it?"' The doctor goes on to talk about his frustration with Jesus raising people from the dead and putting pressure on the health service. The beginnings of this sketch lie in asking, once Jesus has raised someone from the dead, *what next?* Often in comedy you are working forward from an inciting incident and imagining what might happen as a result. Here Palin and Jones imagine what happens after Jesus raises Lazarus from the dead (a subject the Bible apparently doesn't comment on).

Transpositions

We can at this point usefully discuss a pre-*Python* John Cleese and Graham Chapman sketch from a show fronted by Cleese, named *How to Irritate People*. In a sketch in this show, Graham Chapman plays the owner of a car which is faulty, and he has brought it back to the garage. He is the *voice-of-reason*; the car needs fixing and he wants the garage owner to sort it out. The garage owner, played as a 'spiv' incongruously wearing black tie, has an unusual point of view in that he believes he can convince Chapman that there's no problem with the car despite the self-evident issues: it won't start, the brakes don't work, latterly the doors even fall off, clown-car-style. So there are two *points of view* here: *reasonable* and *unreasonable*. This car sketch, written by Cleese and Chapman, had its origins in a real story that Michael Palin had told them about returning an obviously malfunctioning car to the evasive and unhelpful garage owner he'd bought it from. Again, it is a comedy idea drawn from the absurdities of everyday life. Of course, he wasn't as off-the-scale unhelpful as the sketch version: the reality was exaggerated for comic effect (the simplest way of creating comedy), but it has its origins in a real, relatable situation.

In the sketch version there's one *game* being played out: the garage owner refusing to acknowledge there is a problem with a clearly defective car. Both characters stick to their points of view, one reasonable and one not, neither yielding to the other. This is a classic dynamic between comedy characters. When Cleese and Chapman revisited the idea for *Monty Python's Flying Circus*, Chapman felt they could do more with it. In an inspired transposition, Chapman suggested that instead of someone taking a car back to a garage, it could be someone taking a parrot back to a pet shop. Then the question is: what's wrong with it? The answer? It's dead, that's what's wrong with it. They switched the casting here, with Cleese becoming the customer (he'd only spoken an introductory monologue in the car one), with Palin playing the shopkeeper in the same way he played the garage man. Just like the car situation, they are both sticking to their *points of view* and are trying to get what they want. The customer wants redress while the pet shop proprietor just wants the problem to go away.

Despite Cleese's comical behaviour as the customer – as compared to Chapman's restrained, normal performance in the car sketch – he is still the *voice-of-reason*; he has been sold a dead parrot and wants it replaced or to get his money back, and even though the sketch has now gone very far from its origins, and even though Cleese's character is behaving in a very comic and outlandish way, it is grounded in a recognizable dynamic from life. The shopkeeper, like the garage man, is still trying to avoid responsibility. While the main *game* is this dynamic of the pet shop man trying to avoid doing anything about the dead parrot, there's a *sub-game* too. This is John Cleese's customer finding as many different ways as possible to say that the parrot is dead. He employs an increasingly ridiculous series of synonyms for death, doubtless born of the fact that Cleese and Chapman would write with a thesaurus by their side. Notice that this is not simply because to do so is funny; he is trying to solve his problem of getting the pet shop owner to recognize that the parrot is bereft of life. If you'd like to work with this approach, firstly, recall a situation from your everyday life where you experienced bad service. I'm sure that within the last year, you will have experienced service that left you frustrated, confused, angry or even embarrassed. Ideally you will have playfully moaned about the situation already, and so already have a sense of the comic potential. It needn't have necessarily been a big thing: it could just as readily be a small frustration or annoyance. Have you got a bad service example in mind? Exaggerating or heightening the actuality is the first option, but jumping to the transposition phase, what if the self-same bad service played out in another context where it becomes even more ludicrous?

The work–play balance

Back at the British Library, Greg next shows us Palin's handwritten draft of a scene in *Monty Python and the Holy Grail*: 'This is the bit with the coconut shells for the horses,' he says. 'Necessity being the mother of invention, they came up with this very clever way of getting round the fact that they couldn't afford real horses.' This is where the servants of the knights knock two halves of coconut shells together to make the sound of horse's hooves for their masters, who pretend-gallop on mimed steeds. There's no *voice-of-reason* saying it's crazy; we're in a *weird world* where it's just how things are. Greg talks us through the script:

> It begins with this panoramic view of the countryside; mist, music, the sound of hooves coming through. A lot of Palin and Jones's sketches begin with some sort of panoramic shot of the countryside. It seems to be a signature device, and then something very surreal will happen. This one is handwritten but you also get typed scripts in the archive. Michael kept his own copies of

scripts and he often annotated them so you do get variations in the script as it develops: even from a neat, typed copy, he's still working on them.

To illustrate this, Greg showed various versions of the multi-part Spanish Inquisition sketch: 'It's probably my favourite sketch. There are several different versions in the notebooks. Then there's this copy tacked in at the end of one of the notebooks, which is a neater copy, although again it's still got large sections crossed out where they were reworking it.' Whether it's a team or a writing duo, collaborative writing can be highly effective, as it naturally fosters a sense of play and you can divide the work between you. Comedy writing is all about finding the work–play balance, and an effective writing process features a time of play, informal improvisation, either socially or in a writing session, and then careful crafting of the cream of the ideas. The play side of it is ad-libbing, messing around, and then the work side is crafting the best of what's come up. Clearly all play without work is just social banter. But all work without play means you're not tapping into the place from where ideas most naturally emerge. If you work with someone as a pair of writers, like Palin and Jones, this can naturally foster playful improv between you. Cleese and Chapman too made an effective pairing, with Cleese providing the elegant comic structure and Chapman the surreal invention. But don't worry if you're more of an Eric Idle or Terry Gilliam working on your own; even as a solo writer, you can drop into improvising two sides of a dialogue and certainly you can ad-lib a character's speech. If you record yourself doing so, this is the *play* side, then some time later you can listen back to it, creating the distance that a second person would provide as you switch into *work* mode. When the Pythons created their classic material, they would naturally switch from an instinctive flow of ideas to bringing to bear all of their analytical and critical skills to really hone it.

My partner Kate and I collect the humorous (and quite off-the-wall) art books of artist Andrew Lanyon, who is a cousin of Kate's. With something of a Pythonic/ Spike Milligan sensibility, and a madness that is all his own, Andrew draws together words and images to create narratives that weave together art, science, literature, history and sheer absurdity all set in his native Cornwall. When we last met in his Porthleven cottage, I asked him about this work–play balance and he told me:

To break it into two frames of mind is crucial. The inventive and the critical frame of mind. You cannot introduce critical mode into inventive mode; you have to keep them separate. For me, when I have my coffee and marmalade on toast in the morning, the sugar and the caffeine hit, when my brain is fresh, that's when I'm in inventive mode and I produce a load of rubbish because no critical element is allowed to interfere. I'll draw a sketch, shift through images, invent jokes, create narratives. You just run with it and it can go for an hour or three hours sometimes. Critical mode can come later. I have to force myself sometimes to switch modes and to stop inventing. Which can be hard sometimes as I fear if I don't keep inventing I'll lose that ability.

It can be very helpful to look on your comedy work as being in two parts in this way: the 'work and play'. There's the playful phase where you generate ideas and possibilities and more material than you need. This should not be hemmed in by structures or devices or tools, let alone 'rules'. Not even rules of propriety or decency. Let it flow uncensored and unexamined. Then you have the crafting phase where you edit, hone and structure what you've got.

Comedy worlds

When I was growing up, I used to love watching *Last of the Summer Wine* on a Sunday, the *very* long-running British sitcom about three old men gallivanting around in Yorkshire. So long-running was the show that they went through several old men in the three main roles. These central characters are also an example of my boss–striver–fool model that I go on to discuss further in Chapter 8. In the classic line-up you had the *boss* Foggy organizing and taking the lead, Clegg the *striver* and Compo the *fool*. Compo in particular was always getting into scrapes, including a memorable incident involving a bath and a steep hill. In the 'Stop That Bath' episode of series 15, our trio of pensioners are helping a friend wheel a cast iron bath through the streets on a cart. (Don't ask.) As they attempt to push the bath up a steep hill, Compo loses his balance and falls in, at which point the others lose their grip on the cart which then speeds down a hill with an alarmed Compo on board in the bath.

Last of the Summer Wine had an unimaginably long run of thirty-one series; particularly given the single writer, Roy Clarke. This compares to a typical ten to twelve seasons of the longest-running US sitcoms. Meanwhile of course some of the truly classic British sitcoms like *Fawlty Towers* and *The Office* signed off after two series. In 1998, during *Summer Wine*'s prolific run, *The Royle Family* (three series) came out. Created by Caroline Aherne and Craig Cash, it's famously naturalistic and truthful, pioneering the proliferation of brilliant thirty-minute comedy dramas, or 'dramadies', that we enjoy now. Which leads me to compare the worlds of *Last of the Summer Wine* and *The Royle Family* through the lens of old people in runaway baths. While Compo in *Summer Wine* can go down a hill in a bath and bounce back unharmed like a cartoon character, if Nana from *The Royle Family* went flying down a hill in a bath there'd be real consequences. First of all, it's very unlikely to happen, but if the writers did somehow credibly put her into this situation, Nana would probably sustain serious injuries and her family would be deeply worried, perhaps her sanity would be called into question, but it could still be funny in a truthful and poignant way. It would certainly be a climactic event. Maybe a series end. This is a massive thing to happen in a world of everyday, well-observed truthful situations, whereas it's just another routine scrape in *Last of the Summer Wine*.

In the first part of this chapter, we went from Key & Peele to *Fleabag* to *Monty Python*. Due to sharing a heightened, naturalistic, filmic quality, one of the more sketchy scenes from *Fleabag* might not feel too out of place in Key & Peele (the casting notwithstanding). A *Python* sketch, however, would feel jarringly wrong inserted into either show. When you're writing comedy, it's crucial to understand the rules and boundaries of the world you're writing in. Whether it's a world of your own invention, or an existing show you're writing for, you need to consistently get the tone and style right. It'll have its own rules and the audience will have expectations of it that must be respected. To help define your comedy world, I offer my model that places four principle comedy worlds – realist, heightened, cartoon and surreal – around a circle.

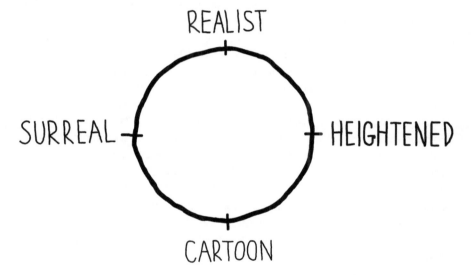

The Royle Family is at the top of the circle in a *realist* world and *Last of the Summer Wine* is diametrically opposite in a *cartoon* world. Furthermore, *The Royle Family* is shot using a 'single-camera' drama production process for a naturalistic effect. *Last of the Summer Wine*, on the other hand, is shot in front of a studio audience, giving the show its laugh track, in quite a theatrical way (with scenes that were filmed on location, like the bath fiasco, being played to the audience on screens). The other main kind of comedy production is the mockumentary, where a documentary production process is used. Knowing which production process you are writing for is important too as they have different demands. (I know from experience that not all new writers have thought about this when they launch into their script.) Broadly speaking, single-camera drama style has to be more truthful and realistic, although you can get an interesting effect if outlandish or surreal content is filmed and acted in a naturalistic way as I discuss below; multi-cam studio audience writing has to be more gag heavy (you have an audience to make laugh!) and as for mockumentary, I'd issue a caution. We have certainly seen a lot of it and it can also be a lazy approach. Characters can speak directly to camera about their thoughts and feelings and you can even have narration making exposition easy to do. I'd only use this format if your idea really requires it. Now let's go round the circle discussing all our areas of comedy: stand-up, improv, sketch and sitcom.

Realist comedy

Typically shot single-cam drama style or mockumentary, with depth and truth; *The Royle Family* is realist as are *Curb Your Enthusiasm*, *The Office* and *This Way Up*, which we talked about in Chapter 1. Since this model is a circle, comedies can be placed in intermediate spots. For instance, I'd place the US *Office* moving round towards *heightened* (see below) as, unlike the UK original, it's more evident it's a sitcom – you'd be unlikely to mistake it for a documentary in the way that some people initially did with the UK original. A stand-up in this real world is very honest and self-revealing. I'm thinking the likes of Richard Pryor or Hannah Gadsby in *Nannette*. There's not much sketch around these parts, but for example *Inside Amy Schumer* has realist sketches, as well as more heightened ones. In Chapter 2 we talked about the TJ & Dave style of improv that sits in this world. Their naturalistic, slow-burn truthful work influenced Katy Schutte own improv and she told me that in this style, 'I wouldn't say it's necessarily more advanced, but I think it's rare that you'll get someone who's a beginner improviser who's comfortable enough, and trusting enough, to do that naturalistic style and to trust that it's going to end up in something that might be hilarious or beautiful.'

If your work, of whatever kind, is to be in this realist world, it'll be emotionally truthful, self-revealing, played more naturalistically and, if filmed, is likely to be a single-camera production using drama processes or shot as a mockumentary. It'll be close to reality, there will be laughs of recognition and the world will be believable. The comedy comes from the rightness and the truth of the observations. The believability and credibility of the world must be maintained, so avoid easy laughs that undermine its integrity. When Larry David is in the edit of *Curb Your Enthusiasm*, for example, he takes out the obvious jokes the cast ad-libbed in order to play the longer game of creating a reality that becomes comedically awkward or absurd, and TJ & Dave eschew any kind of chase for laughs, looking on the comedy that does emerge as a by-product of their truthful exploration of the moment, playing rounded and believably motivated characters.

Heightened comedy

As we move around the circle, we're getting further away from reality. The heightened world is a simplified and further exaggerated version of the real world. The laughs are still emotionally truthful and we recognize the world, but it's pushed beyond being straightforwardly authentic. I feel *Fleabag* is in this space with its often heightened comedy and the trademark breaking of the fourth wall as she speaks to camera. *Fleabag* is shot in a drama style without an audience reaction, as is *Peep Show*, which I feel is another 'heightened' show due to being able to hear the characters' thoughts, not to mention the often grotesque situations. In the studio audience style, we find the likes of *Friends*, *Fawlty Towers*, *The IT Crowd*, *Seinfeld* and *The Big Bang Theory*.

More sketch shows begin to crop up in this heightened area, with many Key & Peele and Fry & Laurie sketches for instance playing out here. A lot of improv is played out in this world too, including The RH Experience who I saw perform their *Stuck* show, which is a long-form narrative where the central characters become, as you'd expect, stuck somewhere. The narrative is about them becoming trapped and then endeavouring to get out. The whole thing is very heightened space, there's nothing of the TJ & Dave naturalism for them, and can also become more cartoon at times so they're across that bottom right corner of the circle. Genre improv tends to be in this heightened area, again shading into cartoon, as Katy Schutte said, 'Murder mystery improv tends to be a little bit camp or elevated, the Agatha Christie type experience, or if you're doing Scandi Noir it'll be more silent and brooding.' Heightened worlds all.

Cartoon world

Despite the phrase 'cartoon world', I'm not referring to animation here (animation can play out in any of the worlds); instead I'm meaning a caricature world, exaggerated and simplified. We're now further away from the real world than ever. We're in *Last of the Summer Wine* territory. Other comedies and comedians here include *Father Ted*, *Toast of London*, Steven Wright, Milton Jones, Demetri Martin and Howie Mandel (see p. 101). The *Mr. Show* 'Burgundy Loaf' sketch (see p. 84) lies here, as do many *Monty Python* sketches; for example , in series 3 of *Flying Circus* they have a brilliant beauty pageant send-up where the contestants, instead of competing on physical attractiveness, are instead being judged on their ability to summarize Marcel Proust's multi-volume masterwork

Remembrance of Things Past. Stylistically it's very cartoon in tone, which for comparison is entirely unlike the realist/heightened *Mr. Show* 'Prenatal Beauty Pageant' sketch. Reminiscent of Chris Morris in tone, in this pageant, pregnant women's foetuses are scanned, with the image projected on a big screen in front of the audience to have their beauty judged. In order to win, parents pay for their foetuses to have beauty treatments including make-up and false eyelashes, which are applied in the womb by a maverick surgeon who says it raises the unborn baby's self-esteem. If you watch these two beauty show sketches side by side, the difference in the worlds is starkly illustrated.

When I asked Katy Schutte to give me examples of improv in this world, she said, 'My brain went to hectic and crazy physical things. Someone might be jumping out of a plane into a car and then driving off a cliff. It can be this awesome fun roller coaster. People like Craig Uhlir [of iO Chicago] who will do very crazy shows. He'll be sweating for an hour, running around and doing a lot of physical offers. With students, the technical problem with this is they can't handle all of the offers yet because it's pretty fast.'

Surreal world

We have now left the real world. Anything can happen. The action doesn't have to conform to any kind of everyday reality. It's a dream world. As an audience, we have to suspend our disbelief to accept the reality of these worlds. My litmus test for whether a show is truly surreal is this: can you have talking animals or objects in the show? If not, it's not fully surreal. This by the way is personification, which we explore in Chapter 8. Comedies operating here are wild outliers. A challenge with sustaining them is as soon as anything can happen it's hard to keep surprising the audience. Here we have *Monty Python* again, *The Mighty Boosh*, Steven Wright again, Eddie Izzard and Noel Fielding. If the *Last of the Summer Wine*'s 'old man going down a hill in a bath' scenario was to happen in a surreal world comedy, it could play out like this:

> On the way down the hill the bath hits a sheep which is sent flying into the sky. Suddenly the bath hits an upward slope and itself takes off and flies into the sky. The old man can't stay in the bath and falls out. But luckily, he lands on a cloud. Which turns out to be the sheep. We watch in terror as the sheep plummets to earth with the old man clinging onto its wool. But luckily the sheep sprouts wings and, with the old man on its back waving cheerfully goodbye, it flies off over the horizon.

A fertile point of the circle is the north-west corner, where surreal begins to shade back into realist. Here you can have something that's really strange and obviously very unreal, but you play it very truthfully. This is a niche area for comedy to operate: see the sketch series *Big Train* and the vampire mockumentary *What We Do in the Shadows*. Stand-ups that operate here include Mitch Hedberg and at times Maria Bamford. Sci-fi comedy can be around this corner, like *Red Dwarf* and Armando Iannucci's space comedy *Avenue 5*. Katy Schutte touched on sci-fi improv: 'Me and my friend Chris do improvised science fiction and we might be in the "north-west".' Good science fiction has believable, relatable characterization, alongside bizarre impossible things.

Going round the comedy worlds circle

In Chapter 1, I spoke with Clelia Mountford, the co-founder with Sharon Horgan of the production company Merman. The work they are most known for has tended to be particularly *realist* in tone. I asked Clelia about their preference for naturalistic and truthful shows and whether they would ever move round my comedy circle to do, for instance, a broad, studio audience sitcom in a cartoon style. She said:

> I haven't really done very broad comedies where gags drive character and story. I'm interested in character first and then developing a story from the character. Then the jokes come in. It's observations from life. Saying that, I think we will possibly do some more heightened comedy because we like silly as well and it makes us laugh. I mean I love *The IT Crowd*. That did it in an interesting way. It depends how it was done. We haven't found the writers who want to do that and we haven't found the story we want to tell. But both of us say we'll never rule it out because we are hungry and greedy and we want to make a lot of things.

In Chapter 7 I speak with Meg Salter who with Janine Harouni and Sally O'Reilly make up brilliant sketch group Muriel. They made their name making online comedy sketches and now they are developing their 30-minute narrative comedy writing, both individually and as a group. When they write sitcom collaboratively, they have a dilemma that this model sheds light on and can help them with. Meg told me, 'When it comes to sitcoms we all have very different ways we naturally pitch things. I'd say Janine's very *Brooklyn Nine-Nine* [cartoon], Sally is *Gavin and Stacey* [realist] and I'm somewhere in between [heightened]. Your circular model is very helpful. We all have to agree where we're writing beforehand, then we're definitely on the same page.'

The first task, then, is to define your comedy world. Secondly, you can consider an idea you have for your piece and test to see if it fits in the world, and if not you can ask how it can be angled to sit within it. For example, I was once working with someone on their sitcom script, set in an office, and they had the idea of someone in the office dying at their desk and, because the person had been so inert and ineffectual, no one noticing for a week. It felt like a funny idea, but a stretch for the heightened world they were operating in. This could work in a surreal or cartoon world, but I felt the idea breaks down if you go into the heightened realm and it simply wouldn't be credible for a reality world; it would be impossible for this to believably happen in *The Office*, for example. It was, however, based on a true story! In the real situation, the person died at their desk late on a Wednesday night and wasn't discovered until the following morning. Now this is credible – it also literally happened. So you'd probably simply stick with the truth for a reality world. In their heightened world you may want to exaggerate: say make it over the weekend or at a push the Christmas break, but you'd keep it believable. So once you have defined the world of your show, you can test the ideas you have to see if they fit the world, and you can take steps to address the issue if not.

A little while ago, I read a sitcom script written by two improvisers moving into scripted comedy which featured a therapist who I felt simply wasn't credible. No real-life therapist would be so irresponsible and ignorant of their field. When I put this to them, their response was 'It doesn't matter if it's funny.' This felt to me like an attitude that was a hangover from their improv work, where indeed it probably wouldn't matter. In improv, as you can't be expected to be an expert on every subject that comes up, there is a high tolerance of experts talking nonsense ands of course your gobbledegook version of their expertise can be hilarious. In scripted comedy different expectations are at play. For one thing, you have had time to look things up! I discussed this unbelievable therapist with Katy Schutte. A likely scenario in improv is that everyone would go along with the nonsense; however, a player might choose to call them out on it and how that might play out is dependent on where you were on the circle. As Katy responded, 'On your circle as you go from the more truthful end of improv to the wackier end of improv there'd be a change in the response. If you're doing the more TJ and Dave stuff, you wouldn't put up with a therapist being unbelievable. You would take that response of "I'm sorry, can I see your qualifications because this doesn't sound like any therapy I've had before?" The client might leave or the therapist might lose their job. Or if you were UCB trained, you'd find "the why" [see p. 32–33]: "Okay, let's investigate how they managed to do therapy in the first place, let's answer that question." Whereas, if you're doing the wacky end or the short form stuff, you'd just be like, "Yes, this is how therapy works now in our world."'

The importance of credible expertise or accurate information does change as you go round my comedy worlds circle. The show the improvisers had written was set in a heightened world, a world that while broader than a realist world still needs to be grounded and believable. Given the tone of the piece, they were at risk of undermining the credibility of the whole situation if we simply don't believe this therapist could actually operate like that and stay in business (or even get started in the first place). Where your comedy falls on this circle will determine how truthful and accurate you have to be. In the realist world, it has to be very credible and accurate – the therapist would have to be believably bad and unprofessional – and it certainly still has to be plausible in the heightened world. But as you move around the circle the importance of accuracy lessens.

If their therapist were in a cartoon world, you could even have a therapist who hurls a wellington boot at their clients' heads to 'knock the bad thoughts out'. That would be much more of a stretch in a realist world, but maybe it could happen if played truthfully. As Katy comments, 'If you're at the TJ & Dave point on the circle you might say to the person having the therapy, "You know this therapist is bullshit?" and they could be like, "Yes, I know it's bullshit, but weirdly I find it really helpful. I think in ten years this will be legit, but, right now, I don't know, I find wellingtons hitting me in the head just takes me out of my problems you know, man." You can choose whether to reject it or justify it, but again truthfully.' When you travel round the circle to the surreal world, all bets are off. You can do whatever you like. The game of the scene could be that the therapist is a Spanish slug. Then as you approach the real world again, that north-west corner, you can start to truthfully play the challenges of having an Iberian slug therapist.

Having discussed the games you play in your comedy and the worlds it can all play out in, we'll next turn to structure. We'll take in sketches, scenes and routines across these upcoming chapters, going on to look in detail at how characters interact in comic scenarios and ending this section with contemporary internet sketches as we explore high-concept 'what if' scenarios.

Chapter 5
SREP: Set-up, Reveal, Escalation, Payoff

Set-up/payoff, the simplest comic structure, is the territory of the one-liner gag or the quickie sketch. You do something to prepare the ground (set-up), then you deliver the words/action/facial expression/pratfall etc. that is aimed to trigger the laugh (payoff). With *Monty Python* still in mind from the previous chapter, the first set-up/payoff example that occurs to me is the 'Fish Slapping Dance'. In the *set-up*, there are two men, John Cleese and Michael Palin, dressed in safari outfits and pith helmets, who are standing facing each other at a lock on a canal (Teddington lock in west London to which I actually made a pilgrimage when I lived out that way). Cleese stands still while Palin dances before him to cheerful music, periodically slapping Cleese across the cheeks with two small pilchards. The music stops and Palin stops dancing, at which point we get the *payoff*. Cleese produces a huge trout he has been concealing from us and with careful precision clouts Palin with it, sending him plunging into the water of the lock. He then strikes a pose and gives a satisfied look to the camera. Despite the 'Fish Slapping Dance' being a world we have never encountered before, the set-up does create expectations. Following Palin's dance and dainty slapping with small fish you would reasonably expect Cleese to respond in kind. This expectation is radically subverted by the payoff, where Cleese produces a huge fish and, instead of a dainty slap, delivers a heavy blow to Palin who plunges several feet into the water below (an unexpected depth for Palin as during rehearsals the water level was higher). Where the set-up creates expectations that are to be confounded by the payoff, this is known as *misdirection*. With the 'Fish Slapping Dance' in mind, I decided to relate all of our opening comedy examples in this chapter to water. To begin with, here's a sweet playground joke you might remember from your childhood or from a Christmas cracker:

Why can elephants swim whenever they want? They always have trunks with them.

These traditional jokes are often in question-and-answer format, where the question is the set-up and the answer is the payoff. In the original version if you don't know the joke, when you hear the set-up your reaction is likely to be 'Huh?' That's the reaction the joke teller wants. You are momentarily puzzled and then the payoff resolves your puzzlement in a pleasingly unexpected way. So for the listener it's a 'Huh? . . . Ah!' experience. In this joke we also of course enjoy (or maybe groan at) the silly wordplay and the idea that an animal would need to wear swimming trunks. A simple way to make it sound more modern (but no less corny) is to make it first person in stand-up style:

> The elephants I saw at the zoo can swim whenever they want. They always have trunks with them.

This version also introduces *misdirection*. When the stand-up says 'The elephants I saw at the zoo can swim whenever they want', your reaction is less likely to be bafflement and more likely to be the assumption that the elephants have a pool of water in their enclosure. Then the pleasure of the payoff is this assumption being confounded. So it's less 'Huh? . . . Ah!' and more 'Yep . . . Oh!' Here's a misdirection joke from stand-up and now musical comic Richard Lindesay (who we met in Chapter 3). To get the most out of this joke you need to know that Richard is, by his own admission, a little rotund.

> I like to do my bit to prevent rising sea levels. By staying out of the water. Every little helps.

We assume of course that when he says he likes to 'do his bit to prevent rising sea levels' that he is talking about taking fewer flights or something of that sort, an assumption that is confounded by the very literal payoff. In a quick sketch from *Smack the Pony*, the misdirection is non-verbal like the 'Fish Slapping Dance', albeit in an everyday world. In the set-up we see Doon Mackichan warming up athletically by the side of a swimming pool (very convincingly, as she is in real life a cross-channel swimmer). Then she steps to the side of the pool . . . and timidly flops into the water where she thrashes about doing a hopeless doggy paddle. Her athleticism in the set-up is misdirecting us to assume the character is a strong swimmer.

In improv, misdirection can play out when a single speaker artfully, in the moment, leads the audience one way and then flips it. However, it can also play out between people. For example, from their performance we the audience assume a relationship between two players of mother and son. To keep it on topic, let's say the two players have begun acting as mother and adult son on a visit to the swimming pool. There could already be some fun here with the mother treating her grown-up son Sam like a little boy, but crucially without yet referring to each other as 'mum' or 'son'. They just have the energy and interactions of that relationship. Then a third player enters the scene and she endows them with the roles of boss and employee (with a weirdly close familial relationship): 'Hello boss, sorry I'm late. Who's doing the lifeguard shift this morning? Me or Sam?' The assumption we had of the situation now has to be radically revised.

SREP in improv, sketch and sitcom

My model of how sketches, scenes and routines unfold is *set-up–reveal–escalation–payoff*. This has become the standard model on the BA Comedy Degree at Bath Spa University that I helped develop and teach on. Pat Welsh, who created the degree, has taken to calling this 'SREP' (pronounce it 'syrup'). 'Remember your SREP', he'll say, and I have adopted this neat contraction. In summary, when you're developing a sketch, scene or a routine, it can be useful to follow this SREP structure:

SET-UP: Establish the who/where/when/what of the situation.

REVEAL: Introduce the game, the comic idea, of the scene.

ESCALATION: Play the game, heightening the comic idea you have revealed.

PAYOFF: The sketch, scene or routine ends, ideally on a surprise.

In the swimming pool scene I began to describe above, the *set-up* misdirects us as to the relationship between the man and the woman who, by their behaviour, seem to be mother and son. In the *reveal*, our third player enters – let's call her Allegra – and we discover they are actually the pool boss and a lifeguard who have this weird mother–son dynamic. Having discovered the game of the scene, we now escalate it. I am enjoying thinking about where this scene could go. Let's say it's Sam's turn to be the lifeguard, and he is being embarrassed in front of Allegra because their boss, behaving like his mother, is concerned about the frightening height of the lifeguard's chair and keeps asking if he has had a 'pee-pee' before starting his shift. Allegra could start teasing Sam, and the boss could treat the whole situation *as if* it's a playground spat and tell Sam that Allegra is just a bully and he should ignore her, while licking a corner of her hanky to dab a little sleep from his eye.

When you have a clear game and a dynamic between the characters, *and you stick to the truth of the interaction*, the scene starts to play, or write, itself. The shared understanding of the improvisers, once they have clicked into the dynamic, will enable them to play it out unplanned, and for a writer it'll guide the scripting of the scene. How to end the scene? I picture Sam getting more and more frustrated and embarrassed at the boss's behaviour until finally he cracks . . . and starts crying *as if* he's a child. His boss (I almost typed 'his mother') takes him into her arms and soothes him. This is the *payoff*.

Sometimes a sketch is a one-off but often a character will recur across a sequence of scenes. This is the beginnings of sketch shifting into longer narrative like a sitcom. A sequence of sketches can be looked upon as building in the same way as a single sketch.

SET-UP – the first in the sequence introducing the character and their behaviour.

REVEAL – the second one can be fairly similar, it is a 'reveal' in the sense that it is revealing that it's going to be a runner.

ESCALATION – The sketches need to keep moving, getting more extreme and being surprising as we go through the sequence.

PAYOFF – The last one that provides a final twist.

The challenge with running sketches is for all the subsequent sketches to do essentially the same thing as the first one but in as many different ways as you can think of. With our swimming pool sketch, we'd want to keep revisiting the boss and the lifeguard with their oddly maternal relationship with Allegra teasing them. What else happens with mothers and their young kids in swimming pools? Maybe the next one could be Sam getting changed for this shift and his boss helping him get his trousers off *as if* she's his mother. You don't need to think of entirely new ideas for the characters; you just need to find new ways of playing out what the audience already enjoy about them.

Keeping with our aquatic theme, in a *Saturday Night Live* parody of *Gidget* – the eponymous heroine of surf novels, films and TV in the 1950s and 1960s – Charlize Theron as 'Gadget' and Taran Killam as Darren are surfing together (achieved using a green screen background). As they surf, Gadget is lamenting the fact that she is soon to go home to Chicago and she hasn't kissed anyone on her holiday. Darren responds that it's funny she should say that because he wanted to talk to her tonight. Gadget is thrilled and asks if it'll be just the two of them alone. This is all the *set-up*. In the *reveal*, Gadget confirms this and says that after the bonfire that night . . . she should meet him by the dead whale. Her response is '*What?*' – which is exactly how you would reply if you were hit by this curve ball. They have now revealed the game of the scene. The troubling reality of a beached whale is transposed into this innocent bubblegum world. The scene *escalates* with Darren explaining that the whale corpse has been on the beach for weeks and is filling up with gasses. Now uncomfortable,

Gadget suggests that maybe they should meet somewhere else. Darren says don't be silly and comes off his surfboard with a cry of 'Wipe out!' And that's the *payoff* of this opening section of the piece. This is less than a minute but here we can see an entire scene playing out as a SREP. It's also of course a parody with built-in assumptions and rules ripe to be sent up, celebrated or subverted.

Sitcom scenes function in the same way as sketches, but they also have the bigger job of threading together a larger narrative across the episode. In a scene from the *Friends* episode 'The One at the Beach', Chandler and Monica are sunbathing and bantering about whether Monica would go out with Chandler if he were the last man on earth (no). Meanwhile, Joey has dug a huge hole that he is proudly standing in. Monica gets up, steps into the sea, and is immediately stung by a jellyfish. This is all *set-up*. Joey then recalls from a TV show on the Discovery Channel that to deal with a jellyfish sting you need to pee on it. This is the *reveal*. Monica is aghast. The situation escalates to the *payoff* where Joey offers the privacy of his large hole for Moncia to do what needs to be done. The game of the next scene (which also has a clear set-up–reveal–escalation–payoff) is a deeply troubled Chandler, Monica and Joey talking to the other Friends about what happened on the beach *as if* they are in a war movie talking about the horrors of combat and the inhuman depths to which they were forced to sink. In the payoff to the scene, we discover that Monica didn't actually pee on her own foot. An initial misdirection makes us think it was Joey until we discover that Chandler did the deed. There is also a sub-game across the two scenes in Joey's obsession with the hole he dug on the beach. And naturally there are the well established character games they all play: Joey being childish, Chandler initially playfully hitting on Monica, Monica being uptight and so on.

Continuing with sitcom, let's look at a *Big Bang Theory* scene from the beginning of the episode 'The Einstein Approximation'. This one has only the most tenuous link to our watery theme. See if you can spot it. In the *set-up*, Sheldon stands with his back to a whiteboard full of equations written in different coloured pens. Every few moments he swings round abruptly, very briefly glimpsing the board out of the corner of his eye. He is clearly behaving unusually. Penny, the voice-of-reason, enters and asks what he's doing. He replies, in the *reveal* of the scene, that he's attempting to view his work as a fleeting peripheral image in order to engage the 'superior colliculus' of his brain. He says he has been up all night, hence acting crazier than normal, and is stuck. Note how Sheldon's strange behaviour is related to him trying to solve his problem; he's not behaving in a randomly strange way. The scene heightens with him running past the whiteboard, swinging his head to one side to briefly glimpse it. Leonard walks in, a second voice-of-reason. Next Sheldon looks directly at the whiteboard but peers through his two clenched fists *as if* looking through a telescope, prompting a Captain Hook gag from Leonard (there it is!). Leonard then suggests Sheldon start again and in the *payoff* to the scene, Sheldon agrees, opens the window and throws the whiteboard out, whereupon we hear the honking of traffic below and the sounds of a car crash.

Live sketch comedy

If you are doing live sketch comedy, you might be presenting sketches on stage in quite a theatrical way, like the Rowan Atkinson example later in the chapter. But if you straddle sketch and improv, and especially if you've been doing stand-up too, you're probably not going to be disappearing behind the fourth wall. No, as in stand-up and improv, you'll be in the same time and space as the audience, acknowledging and playing with the context. And as you will in improv, you'll be having fun with the artifice of the situation, playing with the inherent limitations of performing scenes with not much more than some chairs. In fact, it is this very minimalism which allows you to get quickly in and out of scenarios.

When it comes to the *set-up* of a scene, one of the main challenges with live sketch is conveying the situation without TV's visual cues of sets and costumes. Radio presents similar challenges and so, in a more traditional behind-the-fourth-wall style of sketch, this means the set-up needs to have a lot more verbal information giving the who/when/where/what. You can also use sound effects and music to help establish the situation. However, in the more *stand-up* approach to live sketch comedy, you can simply *tell* the audience what they need to know. For example, with the brilliant lo-fi sketch double-act Two Episodes of Mash, with Joe Wilkinson (himself a stand-up) and Diane Morgan, they casually announce where and when the next scene takes place before they go into it with no theatricality, the characters they're playing essentially no different from their own comedy personas.

In this style of sketch comedy, as exemplified by sketch group Pappy's, about whom Oliver Double writes in the book *Popular Performance*, the whole act will be predicated on the clear comic personas of you and your fellow comics and the relationships between you. And, as can be the case in improv, the characters are often only a thin veil over your own comedic personas. Indeed, the pleasure for the audience will be in seeing *you* playing the characters. And, as when you do a stand-up act-out, you never fully step into a fictional world. Even while a sketch is in progress, you will bicker as 'yourselves' and talk about things that are happening in the room. You might stop a sketch and restart it, or abandon it altogether. None of this need rule out using the formal structures and approaches we are discussing in this chapter, but the great joy of this kind of live work is you can play fast and loose with it all.

SREP in stand-up

Scottish comic Kevin Bridges has a story about being threatened by a knife-wielding man (who he refers to as a 'friendly madman') at a bus stop. In the *set-up*, he gives us the key information – no more and no less than we need to know. He says that it was midnight in Glasgow and that he was at the bus stop with two other people. The set-up can have gags in it, and Bridges finds some laughs here through the unlikely attitude he takes to waiting at a bus stop (he talks about it as if it were a novel and interesting thing to do), but it's primarily doing the job of setting up the who/when/where/what of the story. He also starts with a very different energy from how you'd begin the story in everyday life. He misdirects us. If you were telling a story to your friends and family about being threatened at a bus stop, your energy and attitude from the outset would be telegraphing the fact that it's a dark story. But in stand-up you'll often hide where it's going, as Bridges does here by starting in a light, playful mood. In the *reveal* of the Kevin Bridges bus stop story, after the jovial opening, a threatening madman turns up wielding a knife and says 'Oi fatty', leading Bridges to assess the BMI of the other two at the bus stop only to realize it must be him 'who's about to become a statistic'. Notice how he finds comic angles, or games, to play at every stage of the story. In the *escalation*, the scene heightens with said madman telling Bridges that he'll be stabbed unless he hands over a pound. He reflects on the man's generosity, saving him the hassle of being stabbed and going to hospital for a mere pound. Again, he is taking an unlikely attitude here: one of appreciation and gratitude. The game from that point is Bridges talking about this offer *as if* he is a consumer and the mugger is a salesman: 'I'm a sucker for a bargain', he says. The *payoff* has Bridges reflect that it'd be 'at least a fiver' in Edinburgh.

When I'm teaching stand-up storytelling, another example I like to use is from Kelsey Cook, where she tells the story of an autocorrect error leading to an appalling misunderstanding. In the *set-up* she explains that her childhood cat Cally had died but when she texted her friend Jena to tell her the news – and here's the *reveal* – the autocorrect changed 'Cally' into 'Kelly' – which is the name of their best friend. She lets that sink in. She has important facts to establish clearly at the top, which could be confusing, so watching her take her time to set out the information clearly, while making sure it's understood by the audience, is a great example of a clear, effective set-up. Now she has set it all up, she goes back in time to when she had no idea about this autocorrect error and her appalled friend Jena thinks Kelsey is casually texting about the death of their best friend Kelly, who she's buried in the back yard. This again is *dramatic irony*. (You'll recall that dramatic irony is when the audience knows something, but character(s) in the narrative don't.) A notable aspect of the dramatic irony here is that Cook knows *now* what the problem is, but then goes back in time to when she didn't know. In the *payoff* to the routine, Kelly herself hears of the confusion and is not impressed with Jena's response: 'Thanks for calling the cops, bitch.'

Turning to Richard Pryor's seminal *Live in Concert* show, we find a story of genuine life and death where, with characteristic honesty, he discusses his recent heart attack. I often talk about the effectiveness of raising the stakes in comedy, and here the stakes could hardly be higher. Here's how it unfolds:

Set-up

Pryor opens up the subject by putting a hand to his chest and saying, 'Oh, shit. Had a little pain in my heart there.' He goes on to say he briefly thought he was having another heart attack. This apparent pain in the chest is a very immediate way of introducing the topic. This illustrates something central to stand-up: the topic arises out of the immediate circumstances. The more current a topic feels, and so the more natural it is to talk about it, the more you are concealing the fact that it's all a contrivance to make people laugh. Instead it seems like you are talking about what's on your mind. Pryor goes on to explain that once you've had a heart attack, any little twinge is alarming.

Reveal

He then goes back to the moment when he was having the heart attack and acts it out. This is another strongly 'stand-up' approach. In creative writing (and improv), they have the useful dictum 'show not tell'. In stand-up, you tend to *tell then show*, as Pryor does here. He is now reliving it. Stand-ups will routinely do this, whether it's something as dramatic as a heart attack or something more routine like a date. In this extraordinary *act-out* he says he was walking in the yard when he hears the words 'DON'T BREATHE!' He is startled, and the voice, which we realize is his heart talking, repeats the command.

Escalation

Having introduced the personification of the heart, it toys with him *as if* it's a police officer getting him in a choke hold, which is apt, as he has been speaking about his troubled relationship with the police. With Pryor pleading for his life, he is then told to get down on one knee, which he does both in the story and on stage in front of us. The heart says 'You're thinking about dying now, aren't you?' Pryor agrees that he is. To which the heart says, 'You didn't think about it when you was eating all that pork!' Having played out the personification game, he now moves into the next scene of the story and a new game; an 'as if'. In this second game, he then says that when you're in that position you put in an emergency call to God. Next, he acts out the phone call dialogue: 'Can I speak to God right away, please!' Then he gets put on hold. Here he is acting out a prayer *as if* it's a phone call to a help line. Then the heart gets wind of what's happening and is furious that Pryor is going behind its back to talk to God.

Payoff

I often think of stand-up act-outs as having a documentary approach. You, the comic, are the narrator guiding us in and out of the action. Comedy sketches often have a unity of time and place: they play out in one location in real time, but the flexibility of a stand-up routine readily allows shifts in time and location and multiple games too. Here Pryor jumps forward in time and says he woke up in an ambulance. He looked up to find there was 'nothing but white people staring at me'. There is a touch of misdirection here in that, for a moment, you might imagine he is going to make a comment on the lack of minority ethnic representation in the medical profession. Instead he can't believe he's died and 'wound up in the wrong mother fucking heaven'. More than anyone, I feel Richard Pryor was pivotal to creating the kind of confessional stand-up we enjoy today that almost becomes a kind of therapy.

Ways to escalate a scenario

When you're setting up your own piece, whether it's stand-up, a sketch or a scene in a longer narrative, find the sweet spot between too much and too little information. If there is too much information in the set-up, or irrelevant details, the audience lose the focus. But if there is not enough, they won't know what's going on. It can take some work to get a set-up to be clear and economical. Then reveal the central comic idea in one clean hit. Be clear what the idea is. A confused audience do not laugh. Once you have set up your situation and introduced the game, you're then looking to escalate or heighten it. Here are three approaches you might take: *variations*, *one-upmanship* and *revelations*. Broadly, comic ideas often tend to escalate through one or more of these common devices and one does tend to dominate. (I give sketch examples here, but you can use these approaches in any kind of comedy.)

Variations

The same idea is played in a different way. This is a strongly stand-up approach where the form allows you to keep coming at the same topic from multiple angles. One sketch example, a fantastically anarchic scene from one of the two special *Monty Python* episodes made for German television, has a man wanting to buy a hearing aid but it turns out the shopkeeper is deafer than the customer is. In fact, he's so profoundly deaf he can barely function in his role, but nevertheless he cheerfully attempts to discharge his duty. Then in the escalation we have a variation on the original idea with a new character joining the scene who is an almost entirely sightless seller of contact lenses.

One-upmanship

Keegan-Michael Key, of Key & Peele, says a lot of his favourite sketches are ones where he and his partner Jordan Peele get 'to one up each other'. He says it's not 'arguing and screaming', it's a heightened competitiveness as they each try and outdo the other. He describes it as a 'delicious tension' and more interesting than straight arguing.[1] A classic example is *Monty Python's* 'Four Yorkshiremen' sketch where, famously, the game is them trying to outdo each other in the poverty of their upbringing. For example, in response to someone claiming that when they were young their family lived in a corridor, another says, 'We used to *dream* of living in a corridor! Would have been a palace to us. We used to live in an old water tank on a rubbish tip!'

Revelations

Another way of escalating a sketch is through a series of further reveals. In Rowan Atkinson's live show dating from 1992 there's a sketch where he plays an unreasonable (and alarming) Scottish headmaster to Angus Deayton's reasonable, disgruntled parent, Mr Perkins. Written by Ben Elton and Richard Curtis, it is a great example of escalating a sketch through further reveals. Firstly, the *game* of the sketch is the headmaster being unreasonably blasé about the death of the man's son whilst at school. There are two points of view. The headmaster has an *unusual* perspective and Mr Perkins is the *voice-of-reason* whose confusion and struggle to understand what's going on is a big part of the comedy. The escalation in this sketch is fuelled by misunderstandings and the series of revelations.

The set-up begins by establishing who is who, the context and the fact that Mr Perkins has been called in by the head to discuss his son's recent behaviour. The concerned father listens to the litany of issues: *He seems to take no interest in school life whatsoever. He refuses to muck in at the sports field. And it's weeks since any master has received any written work from him.* Mr Perkins expresses his concern. Then we get the reveal: 'Quite frankly, Mr Perkins, if he wasn't dead, I'd have him expelled.' How does Mr Perkins respond? A less experienced writer

---

[1] J. D. Fox, 'Keegan-Michael Key's 11 Favorite Sketches From Key & Peele's Final Season', *Vulture*, 26 August 2016, https://www.vulture.com/2016/08/key-peele-favorite-season-five-sketches.html.

might have him come back with 'Oh my god! My son is dead!' But this is forcing him too quickly to accept the unusual thing. Instead, he simply comes back with 'I beg your pardon?' – as you would. Then in the first of many misunderstandings the headmaster assumes he's concerned about his son's potential expulsion, not his actual death. The headmaster goes on to give more details: he's lying in the sick bay, stiff as a board and bright green, noting that this is typical of his current attitude. Now the penny drops for the father, who demands to know how he died – a question the headmaster feels is unimportant, but with some prompting he explains that they've had a lot of trouble recently with boys taking out library books without library cards, Mr Perkins's son was caught and the head administered a beating, during which he died. This is escalating the sketch through a second reveal: it was the headmaster that killed the boy.

More misunderstandings follow, culminating in Mr Perkins wanting to know exactly what happened, to which the headmaster (misunderstanding what he's concerned about) responds, 'Well, apparently, boys were just slipping into the library and taking the books!' The conversation becomes more and more ridiculous, building to the head saying that in order to accommodate the funeral, he has had to cancel afternoon school on Wednesday. Finally, Mr Perkins cracks and says, 'This is preposterous!' (again, an entirely plausible reaction), to which the headmaster replies that he has been joking, citing his strange sense of humour. Mr Perkins is naturally hugely relieved. This is a false dawn (see below). He believes at this point that everything is back to normal and his son is still alive. Then the head reveals that what he was actually joking about was cancelling afternoon school – there's no way he'd do that to 'bury that little shit!' – and the father is plunged right back into the insanity.

In a more up-to-date example, I have just watched a *Saturday Night Live* sketch which at the time of writing is brand new this week. The wonderful 'New Paint' sketch, despite at this point being online only for a few days, is approaching two million views. It's a great example of a sketch that, after the opening reveal, escalates though a series of further revelations. The game of the scene is Aidy Bryant's character being obsessed by, and spending a fortune on, Farrow & Ball paints, despite not being in a position financially to do so. It feels like an instant classic. In the *set-up*, the outside of a neat, well maintained suburban house is shown; then we cut inside to an immaculate sitting room with a very striking shade of blue on the walls. Aidy Bryant brings out some posh cheeses and fig jam, already setting up the pretensions of her character, then Beck Bennett says 'Thanks sis', and with his arm around Kristen Stewart he says they haven't visited for ages due to their new baby, thereby setting up the relationships. Stewart says the living room looks amazing and asks if she has painted. She has. Notice how efficiently and painlessly all the background information we need has been put in place. We've been told everything we need to know – no more and no less. Stewart wrongly attempts to guess the maker of the paint and Bryant, as if in a commercial, says that 'in this house I only use Farrow & Ball', the high-end British paint. This is the *reveal* of the sketch, getting the *game* in motion. A *sub-game* also begins as she verbally pronounces the 'u' in the British spelling of the word 'colour'. This sub-game is played throughout, with Bennett taking it on later in the scene. Two *points of view* are established here as the brother and his wife are shocked by Bryant's profligacy.

The sketch *escalates* as Bryant parrots Farrow & Ball marketing speak for the names of her paint and the inspiration for the colours. The next step is the reveal of the (genuine) cost of the paint in the US, including the materials, shipping and the labour (Bryant also pronounces 'labour' with an additional British 'u'). The cost is astronomical, especially given that, as her brother angrily points out, she is an out-of-work day bartender. The sketch then escalates through a series of further *reveals*: it seems she's spent her inheritance on the paint; we discover the place is rented, so she'll have to paint it back when she leaves; a man enters (a new character coming in to heighten the escalation) and we discover she's sleeping with this man whom she met on Facebook Marketplace. This sequence of revelations culminates in her drunkenly saying that the baby is not her brother's and has his wife's 'trainer's eyes'. Bryant says 'Look at the *colour* of the baby's eyes' (of course mispronouncing the word 'colour'). The husband looks closely at the baby's eyes, realizing the significance for the first time, and the two women fight. The *payoff* is the revelation that we have been watching a commercial as a voice-over comes in, over an image of a can of their paint, saying 'Farrow & Ball, each colour tells a story' (and subtly saying 'colour' as Bryant has), the neat implication being that rather more so than the paint on the walls, the baby's eye colour tells a story.

If there's quite a big backstory to your scene, in the same way you can reveal enough at the outset to set the game in motion and then drip out further reveals as it progresses; and in a sitcom or longer narrative, these further reveals might be dripped out across a number of scenes. In improv of course you're actually discovering the 'reveals' as you go, but we suspend our disbelief and play along with the idea that we're being progressively let in on more and more of a pre-existing backstory.

Payoffs

You will have noticed that I tend to use the term payoff for the ending of a sketch or scene, as the word 'punchline' tends to imply a spoken gag while a payoff is not necessarily verbal. The 'punch' also suggests one line or one quick bit of action, whereas sketches can often enter a payoff section that is a number of lines. Here are some common ways of ending sketches, scenes or stand-up routines. If you're stuck for an ending, use this as a checklist.

Reversal (or 'buy in')

This is where the voice-of-reason character suddenly reverses their position to buy into the perspective of the unusual character at the last.

Revelation

The final moment casts everything that came before in a new light. The ending of the 'New Paint' sketch does that when, after a series of revelations, we discover the truth about the parentage of the baby before, in one further flip, it's all revealed to be an unlikely commercial.

New character

Often the comedy comes from the new character having no idea what's just happened, in which case it creates dramatic irony: the audience know something the character doesn't. Or they could join in with the existing unusual character, and the two become peas in a pod. Also, it's worth noting that a new character coming in can often be used midway in a sketch to give escalation more energy (as in the *SNL* 'New Paint' sketch).

False dawn

This is where it seems for a moment that everything is resolved, but then at the last we discover that it isn't. For example, in the Rowan Atkinson headmaster sketch described above. This can also happen midway in a scene to good effect.

Violence

If stuck for something else, have one character punch, shoot or kick the other!

A callback

Something from earlier in the scene is reincorporated at the end.

Here are some further endings that have a particular stand-up flavour but that might also serve you when you're thinking about sketch or scene endings. Many of the endings that follow could potentially involve a callback.

Full-circle

This is a neat ending and definitely involving a callback. With this you take us back to the topic or statement you started with. This, incidentally, is commonly seen in newspaper columns.

Back to the present moment

It can be effective to bring the focus back into the room or the present situation right at the end. For example, if you've been talking about dating, you can end by trying to get a date with someone in the room.

'I'm off to . . .'

End the set by saying you're off to do something related to what you've been talking about. Or even contradicting what you've been talking about.

Call to action

End with an instruction for the audience to follow or a rallying cry. For example, 'So I urge you all, tomorrow morning go up to your boss and tell them where to stick their job.' (The fake TV commercial ending of the 'New Paint' sketch is also a call to action.)

QED

You reach a conclusion based on everything that's been said. You end by saying you've proved your point, maybe with a spurious air of logic or science.

Meta-ending

This self-referential ending is where you step out of the act and refer to the fact that you are trying to end your set. For instance, 'I wasn't sure how to end this bit, but then something happened today that is a perfect example of what I'm talking about.' A meta-ending can also happen in a sketch of course and will routinely happen in *Monty Python*, for example in the Spanish Inquisition sketches we discussed earlier, where the *payoff* to the sequence of sketches is *meta-comedy* where the cardinals are incongruously and anachronistically on a modern-day bus racing to get back to the studio before the programme ends.

In all of the sketches, scenes and routines discussed in this chapter, the funniness is supported by but doesn't, of course, stem from the structure. Indeed, it'd be perfectly possible to have an exemplarily crafted piece that is not at all funny! (Indeed, as I demonstrate in my presenting and speaking training, this self-same structure works with serious content.) The comedy itself comes from characters and their interactions, so that's where we turn next.

Chapter 6
Character Behaviour and Awareness

It used to be routine to talk about the straight man–funny man dynamic in comedy. Aside from the gender assumptions in that term, it's also problematic, as the 'straight' person is a real engine of funniness. That's why, instead of 'straight–funny' I like to think in terms of 'reasonable–unreasonable'. When you have people behaving unreasonably (within which I include inappropriately, idiotically, ineptly, insanely and so on), what we really enjoy is watching reasonable people having to deal with them. It's their reactions to them that often trigger the biggest laughs. Looked at in this way: a lot of your comedy sketches, scenes and routines will boil down to someone reasonable having to deal with someone behaving unreasonably. One is the voice-of-reason that the audience can relate to and, what we might call, a voice of unreason.

Often such scenes are two-handers, but as we see in *Mr. Show*'s 'Burgundy Loaf' restaurant sketch, you can have multiple characters with two points of view in the scene. There are about six unreasonable characters, including the woman diner, and the one squirming, embarrassed, reasonable soul, the male diner. The game of the sketch is that the very fancy restaurant, The Burgundy Loaf, *services their diners' every need at the table*. In the sketch, the *set-up* establishes that we're in a high-end restaurant where a man and woman are on a date and they are finding it all very classy. The man says it's a six-star restaurant, and has been rated the 'ultimate dining experience'. The head waiter comes over to check all is well, and they say they are very happy. Notice the man starts the scene positively. It's always good to give your characters somewhere to fall from. Next, the woman says she will go and wash her hands. She is about to get up when the head waiter stops her and, with a clap of his hands, summons 'le hand-washier'. Whereupon, a man wearing a white jacket appears with a crystal bowl and a towel so she can wash her hands without leaving the table. They are impressed. Then we get the *reveal*, with the man getting up and asking where the 'men's room' is. At which point the head waiter stops him and explains that they would not spoil the atmosphere of the restaurant with 'a men's toilet room'. He claps his hands again and a special, luxurious chair, 'crafted from Brazilian mahogany', is produced that has a toilet seat affixed to it and underneath is a handcrafted, velvet lined wooden box with Italian gold leaf, for the diner to defecate into.

I won't describe the scene in detail, but suffice to say the man is suddenly uncomfortable about all this. His date is fine with it, however, and for the staff this is clearly all normal, so he doesn't protest and (despite his evident discomfort) he sits on the box to do his business as asked. The absurdity is heightened further by him and his date having a normal conversation while he sits on the box, and later with the waiting staff being concerned as to the quality of the evacuation. Finally, after wringing every drop of the man's discomfort out of the scenario, the man has finally finished . . . and the payoff is that they don't have toilet paper (of course). Instead another man is summoned who is incongruously dressed as a chimney sweep and has a cart full of cleaning supplies. The sketch is a favourite of Steve Kaplan's and his brilliant analysis of the scene can be found in his *Hidden Tools of Comedy* book. He told me, 'I always show it in my workshops. It's silly, it's funny, but there's a real predicament. The guy is really embarrassed, but he's got to go through with it because he's a non-hero and his girlfriend seems to think it's okay and you don't know, maybe everybody is doing this at six-star restaurants. How do you know?' It's taking a very recognizable awkwardness and predicament and pushing it somewhere really absurd, but it's grounded in emotion we can recognize.

Regarding the crucial reacting characters, Steve put it this way: 'If somebody's doing something crazy, who's watching that, where's reality? If there's nobody creating reality for me, I don't know what reality is and we're just all floating up into space. It's that old John Cleese quote from Monty Python: "We thought that comedy was watching somebody do something silly. We came to realize that comedy is watching somebody watch somebody do something silly."' The Burgundy Loaf sketch absolutely needs the normal, reasonable customer to be uncomfortable about being asked to defecate into a box at the table. If he was comfortable with it and enjoying the excellent service, we'd get a window onto a weird world but we wouldn't have the enjoyment of watching someone like us struggling with the insanity.

Another way of looking at the unreasonable–reasonable dynamic is *Straight Line–Wavy Line*. This model of Kaplan's has the unreasonable person on a Straight Line trajectory through the scene, as they are unbending in their behaviour. The head waiter expecting the diner to crap into a box in the 'Burgundy Loaf' sketch is a Straight Line as he is unyielding in the disgusting absurdity he is foisting on his customer. Meanwhile, the diner is the Wavy Line as he goes on an emotional journey that takes him from enjoying the evening to the heights of awkwardness, shame and embarrassment. As Steve explains, the Wavy Line is *us*, the audience. They have our perspective in the scene and it is their predicament that we identify with. In another restaurant scene, but this time in realist style, from *Curb Your Enthusiasm*'s 'Denise Handicapped' episode, Larry David is dining with his date Denise and the waiter brings them a piece of pie 'courtesy of Mr. Ted Danson', who is dining with another man elsewhere in the restaurant. Larry and Denise both smile in the direction of Ted at this gesture but agree that they are full and so cannot eat the pie. The waiter politely goes to take the pie away again, at which point a smiling Danson comes over, takes the pie from the waiter, puts it back on the table and tells them how great it is. Larry says he doesn't want dessert, then the mood turns argumentative when Danson says Larry is making him look an 'asshole' and an increasingly vitriolic, profanity-filled argument over the pie ensues, the evening now ruined. Both Larry and Ted are Straight Line characters behaving unreasonably and our Wavy Line characters are the reasonable people, the waiter and Denise, who are stuck between them.

Degrees of awareness and caring

How aware are your characters of how their behaviour is affecting others or how unusual the situation is, and how much do they care? In the 'Burgundy Loaf' sketch, the male diner *is* aware this is an unreasonable situation; however, it's a low-level nagging awareness (rather than a blazing certainty). It certainly *feels* unreasonable, but he is disempowered by the status of the restaurant and its staff, their overbearing manner and the fact that his date is *entirely* unaware there is a problem and is very happy with the service. This is where you want him. If he was convinced in his rightness he would walk out, but we want to see him with a dilemma, stuck in his predicament. Of course, the staff of the Burgundy Loaf restaurant are oblivious to how gross and inappropriate it all is. To them, it's the height of wonderful service. However, sometimes your unreasonable character might be aware that their behaviour is a problem. Let's turn from restaurants to coffee shops, and to another *Curb* episode where a heavily sarcastic Larry David goes into a Starbucks and orders a 'vanilla bullshit latte capa thing'. As is often the case with Larry, he is very much aware of how unreasonable his behaviour is *and he doesn't care*. So, with your unreasonable characters, if you grant them some awareness then the next question is . . . do they care? The degree to which your characters care can be a key part of the comedy. You have Larry David in *Curb* not caring enough about social niceties and conversely in *Friends* Monica cares too much about small things.

Friends features many interactions (in effect quick sketches) where in the Central Perk coffee shop the reasonable customers are having to deal with the unreasonably incompetent waitress Rachel. Her bad waitressing is a running joke across episodes, but at its heart is the self-same dynamic as the 'Burgundy Loaf' sketch: reasonable people wanting to be served and being unreasonably treated. Often, she is fully aware of her bad service and doesn't care. For example, when Ross keenly asks for a foppish sounding pie, she simply responds with a withering look and Ross withdraws the order. The big difference, however, is the comedy world it plays out in. In my terms, *Friends* is a *heightened* world and the 'Burgundy Loaf' is *cartoon*. To appreciate the difference, it would be unthinkable in *Friends* to have Rachel forcing a patron at Central Perk to shit into a box!

So, we've seen:

- characters behaving unreasonably who are *unaware* they are doing anything wrong;
- and characters behaving unreasonably who *are* aware but don't care.

Then you might have:

- characters who are behaving unreasonably *and* they are aware of it *and* they care.

For example, in another interaction with Rachel in Central Perk, a customer points out her incompetence and she says she feels she's getting better (set-up). Whereupon she turns round and asks, 'Does anyone want coffee?' and *everyone* in Central Perk raises their hand (payoff). The joke here hinges on Rachel not being aware in the set-up and then being aware *and caring* in the payoff. Characters who are flawed, yet aware of it and struggling to be better, can be very likeable to an audience, for instance Sharon Horgan and Rob Delaney's characters in *Catastrophe*. These characters care and want to be better, but keep tripping themselves up.

Continuing with the coffee theme, in the sitcom *Miranda*, the eponymous character and her mother are in a taciturn psychiatrist's office. Miranda helps herself to coffee from a machine (noting that the powerful jet reminds her of a urinating horse), proceeds to sit down and then spills the boiling hot coffee into her lap. She leaps up and takes off her soaked trousers, then to protect her modesty she proceeds to wrap herself in the psychiatrist's expensive 'silk-mix throw' (ignoring his protestations), which she uses as a sarong. The game of the scene is Miranda wanting to prove her sanity, but increasingly suggesting the opposite while the deadpan psychiatrist looks on. She is aware how strangely she is coming across *and* really cares about it, but can't help herself. A great *Smack the Pony* sketch is a reverse of this scenario where it's the medical professional who is behaving unreasonably: Sally Phillips plays a doctor who has just explained to Fiona Allen's sniffling patient that she is prescribing her a placebo. The patient is puzzled as to how that would help and the doctor explains that if the patient believes it to be an active drug then the non-active placebo can have an effect. When the patient points out that she's just been *told* it's a placebo, the suddenly panicked doctor tries all sorts of ways to trick her into believing it's a real drug, painfully aware of her predicament.

To further consider the question of how aware characters are and if they care, let's turn to one of my favourite *A Bit of Fry & Laurie* sketches. In the *set-up* a man is making a report to a police officer at the front desk of a police station and when the officer asks his name, he (unreasonably) responds, 'My name is Derek . . .' and then drops a lighter onto the counter. Yes, the sound of the lighter hitting the counter is his surname! That's the *reveal*. The game of the sketch, then, is the reasonable policeman trying to write down this impossible name. As the scene *escalates*, the policeman is initially baffled – as you would be: 'Derek (DROPS LIGHTER) is your name?' Generally, you want your voice-of-reason character to have a period of confusion where they try and get their heads round the strange situation they suddenly find themselves in. If they too quickly accept the premise, their journey through the sketch lacks credibility and it feels like they are just there to facilitate the strangeness of the other character (for more on this, see p.94). Having established that the lighter-drop is indeed the man's surname, in an inspired exchange, the policeman asks how you spell the name and the man responds, 'It's as it sounds.'

After much toing and froing with the name, they move on to the address, which in a variation of the original idea has a physical action in it. He says his address is 'Number 22', and then does a little tap dance which ends with him giving the officer a light slap on the cheek. He concludes the address with 'King's Lynn'. If you don't know the sketch, really you have to watch it but hopefully you get the idea. The police officer naturally reacts very sternly to being struck in this way, but the man protests his innocence. He doesn't understand what the police officer's problem is: it's just his address! The sketch has a three-beat *payoff*: the policeman suddenly accepts that the address can have a dance and a slap to the face in it, but when he reads it back, because he can't read his handwriting, the dainty slap the man gave him suddenly becomes a punch to the man's face. That's beat one. It's a *reversal* in that the voice-of-reason policeman is taking on the behaviour of the unusual character. The man is shocked and the policeman responds, consulting his notes, 'Do you know from some angles it almost looks like . . .', at which point he does the little dance again and unexpectedly produces a cricket bat that he uses to whack the man round the head. Beat two, then, is a violent ending. Now we reach the third beat of this payoff and this time it's a meta one. Meta-comedy is when the artifice is suddenly acknowledged and the performers step out of the fiction to talk directly about the performance they are engaged in. Here Hugh Laurie says, in response to the blow, 'That was too hard', which Fry's policeman pooh-poohs, and Laurie then adds 'Never mind the frigging sketch that was too hard . . .', to which Fry responds, 'Ahhh, diddums,' and then to camera, 'He's just a child really.'

The man with the strange surname and address in the Fry & Laurie sketch has no idea he is behaving unreasonably. In his mind, he's entirely in the right and it's the policeman that's at fault. He's unaware and so can't care. The policeman as the voice-of-reason knows the behaviour is wrong and he does care about it being done properly. If he didn't care, and just accepted a name with the sound of a lighter being dropped, you don't have any conflict and no scene. Later, and this is one of the reasons this is an interesting one to pick, he takes on the unusual behaviour of the other character – when he repeats his address with the tap dance and slap; and then escalates it to a tap dance and a whack round the head with a cricket bat – here he is aware that his behaviour is inappropriate and he doesn't care! Then the third level of awareness and caring is suddenly revealed when they make the meta-comedy switch and break out of the scene and speak to the audience as 'themselves'. Here they are both aware that Stephen Fry the actor has apparently got carried away with how hard he has hit Hugh Laurie, and Laurie cares but Fry doesn't! It can be fruitful as you write to track who is aware and who cares at different points in a scene or narrative.

At the end of this sketch, then, Fry & Laurie step out of role to be themselves (or at least their comedic selves). In Amy Schumer's 'Last Fuckable Day' sketch, all the actors in the scene are playing versions of themselves, as Larry David and Ted Danson do in the scene we discussed earlier. The Amy Schumer sketch also introduces another aspect of comedy writing. It's an example of satire, whose targets are powerful, where the issue is topical and the writers have a strong opinion to express. The sketch is *set up* by Schumer stumbling upon Tina Fey, Julia Louis-Dreyfus and Patricia Arquette sitting around a table having a picnic. There is humour in the set-up, in that Louis-Dreyfus recognizes Schumer as 'the girl from the television who talks about her pussy all the time', and Schumer is amusingly touched by this. The game is *revealed* when the picnicking older actors say they are having the picnic to celebrate Louis-Dreyfus's 'last fuckable day'. As the scene *escalates*, they explain to the younger Schumer that 'in every actress's life, the media decides when you've finally reached the point where you're not believably fuckable anymore'. Everyone at the table nods sagely in agreement.

In Schumer's sketch she plays the innocent voice-of-reason, questioning what the more worldly older actors say (and that's the two points of view: innocence and experience). Having Schumer not know about this day enables her to ask questions and for the other women to elaborate. Early on Fey says, 'You know how Sally Field was Tom Hanks's love interest in *Punch Line* and then, like, twenty minutes later, she was his mom in *Forrest Gump*?' Later in the sketch, in response to Schumer asking if men in Hollywood have a 'last day' too, we learn: no, they don't! Apparently, Bruce Willis is engaged to a female so young she's an 'actual baby lamb'. The *payoff* to Schumer's sketch is also in three beats like the Fry & Laurie one. We cut to a different setting later in the day and Louis-Dreyfus is now in a rowing boat. The first gag is a misunderstanding joke. Schumer thinks they are going to kill her with a bow and arrow, but it turns out that what she sees is an oversized novelty lighter, and they are merely lighting her fat celebratory cigar. Then the second beat of the payoff is a callback: in this case, the rumour from earlier that Bruce Willis is literally dating a baby lamb is, via a phone update, confirmed as true. Then the third beat to the payoff has Fey saying she is off to wax her beard. Naive to the last, Schumer strokes her chin and asks when that happens. The actors in Amy Schumer's sketch are clearly aware of their position in Hollywood, but the fact that it's played like they don't care (or at least they are accepting that this is simply how things are) is a big part of the funniness. If they were angry or insecure or campaigning it'd lose a lot of the humour. (To be clear, the writers and performers themselves care passionately, which is why they made the sketch. It's just funnier if the characters are dispassionate.)

Writers rooms

On a side note, this great *Inside Amy Schumer* sketch emerged from a collaborative writers room context, so I wanted to take a brief detour to further discuss this kind of writing process that we first touched on with *Broad City* in Chapter 1. It's less common in the UK, but standard practice in the US. At its best, the writers room can have the energy of a bunch of friends hanging out and inspiring each other, with the discipline to capture the best of the ideas and make them into a script. Comedian and author Samantha Irby was invited to join the writers room adapting Lindy West's uproarious memoir *Shrill* into a comedy series for Hulu. Annie, the central character in the show, is trying to make it as a journalist. While the world around her judges her because of her weight, she becomes determined to change her life without changing her body. New to the writers room process, Samantha described it as 'hanging out with your friends in the same room every day, arguing about what should happen on a show you haven't watched yet'.[1]

   With the 'Last Fuckable Day' sketch, Schumer says that the conversation in the writers room began by discussing how in movies, as she puts it, 'some sixty-five-year-old dude is with Natalie Portman or the other one who looks like her, and the audience are meant to coo "Oh, they're in love."' Jessie Klein, an American writer, actress and stand-up comedian from New York City, says that this conversation, about how women end up 'ageing out of Hollywood', moved on to asking: do they know exactly when the transition happens? The thought came up that there must be a moment, a single day, and then, as she puts it, 'the phrase "last fuckable day" came out of someone's mouth'.[2]

[1] S. Irby, 'I had zero experience in a writers' room. Then I was offered my dream job in LA', *Guardian*, 14 March 2020, https://www.theguardian.com/media/2020/mar/14/writers-room-dream-job-la.
[2] 'See Amy Schumer Explain "The Last F**kable Day", *Tribeca Talks*, 20 April 2015, https://www.youtube.com/watch?v=0mg78OdhAe0.

Neil Casey has been a writer for both *Inside Amy Schumer* and *Saturday Night Live* (*SNL*), so when we spoke, I took the opportunity to ask him about the difference between working in a writers room on a show like *Inside Amy Schumer* and the distinctive *SNL* approach. He told me:

> It's the difference between pre-taped and cable at *Schumer*, versus live and network at *SNL*. At *Schumer* we had months to write and rewrite and then finally produce these sketches. Whereas in *SNL*, everybody's just barrelling towards the finish line all week, and then the show goes on at 11.30 pm and that's it. Compared to *SNL*, Schumer is a much more collaborative environment. I came in on season 2, so I was lucky enough to have a season 1 as an example of what works. You know who your star is, and you want to play to their strengths. I went in and pitched stuff just based on what we were talking about in the room or what was going on in the news. You'll pitch an idea, you'll riff with the room, and then you continue to own the sketch, go home, rewrite it a couple of times and then bring it back to the table. You're getting feedback the whole way. I think that it shows in the final product.

He went on:

> A difference for me with *SNL* is I was a junior writer, so I was writing a lot by myself in a room with a closed door, and then it would sink or swim at the table. You climb a real hill there every week. You write four or five things, but only two of them are actually even going to be read at the table, and then maybe one of them will make it to the dress run through and zero will make it to air. That's a pretty normal week for a lot of the writers there. With the breakneck pace that things get made and put on the air, it's thrilling when it succeeds. You wrote this thing Tuesday night, and now you're standing behind the camera and the camera turns red, and seven million people are watching it. There's nothing else like it. It's incredibly fun. Then you have one day off and then you're back on Monday to do it all again. I loved it in many ways but, especially as I barrel into middle age, showing up at 10.00 am with a cup of coffee and musing on a sketch all day and then shooting something five months later is a pretty good game.

Reasonable and unreasonable behaviour in transaction scenes

When I'm teaching sketch writing, I often get the students improvising shop or service sketches (for example a newsagent or a dry cleaners). Often with a bit of stopping and starting and nudging in the right direction, the best of them become strong, written sketches. Improv is also a great tool for you to experience, moment by moment, what keeps a sketch on track and what can derail it, and of course if you are an improviser this work will help develop your skills for character interaction in scenes.

Shop sketches would be termed in improv circles, 'transaction scenes'. These are often seen as pitfalls for the improviser for the very good reasons that the characters are strangers, they have no emotional relationship and the scene can easily end up revolving around talking about the *thing* of the scene. However, as improv teachers will point out, these kinds of scenes can work in the right hands and sometimes it's suggested that if the customer and shopkeeper know each other and have a pre-existing emotional dynamic, that can be a way round the pitfalls of the transaction scene. Another suggestion is that the scene be about something other than the actual product or service that is the focus of the transaction. These suggestions are both sound, but certainly in written sketches, and with skilled improv players too, it *is* possible to produce an engaging funny scene from a shopkeeper and customer who don't know each other and are in a dispute over the product. In fact, if you are moving into writing sketches from an improv background, I would urge you to shake off any aversion you have developed to them and to embrace writing transaction scenes! They are a great training ground for sketch writing.

Since the shop assistant/customer roles are so familiar to us, even non-improvisers, with some guidance, can readily improvise such a scene. Here's how it works. There'll be two players. The scene can take place in any kind of shop or service situation, but let's do a shop. Here are the two versions:

1   The customer wants something *reasonable* and is being *unreasonably* blocked by the shop assistant.

2   The customer wants something *unreasonable* and is being *reasonably* blocked by the shop assistant.

Let's play option 1. The *Monty Python* Parrot sketch is of this kind, where Cleese's customer entirely reasonably expects something to be done about the fact that the parrot he purchased is dead, while the pet shop man unreasonably denies there is a problem. Another example is a sketch from Chris Morris's radio show *Blue Jam*, where David Cann plays a man, aged forty-five, quite reasonably trying to buy a case of wine from an off-licence from a young man (played by Kevin Eldon) working there who unreasonably refuses to serve him in the mistaken belief that he's not old enough to buy alcohol (he thinks he's seventeen). They up the ante by Cann having important guests for dinner that evening. The game of this sketch is to try to buy a case of wine from someone who (wrongly and absurdly) doesn't believe you're old enough. Now you might ask yourself in your own sketch, why does the unreasonable character hold their point of view? Often, as in this *Blue Jam* sketch, they just do. You don't need to explain it or justify it. It's not as if the man looks young. As he says himself, 'I'm quite clearly forty-five. Look at the grey hair.' While the *Python* pet shop man is aware his behaviour is unreasonable, as his shiftiness attests, the youth serving in the off-licence is absolutely unaware he is behaving unreasonably. He is just carrying out his job in a rather bored way. To him, he's just dealing with another underage boy trying to buy alcohol. (In response to the grey hair comment he responds, 'It could be make-up.') It's a great sketch for following the emotional journey of the reasonable character through the scene; he begins politely asking for a case of wine, then is confused by the lad's belief that he might be under age, then he becomes impatient, then he tries to bargain with him and finally he becomes furious and starts swearing (to which the off-licence youth wonders aloud what his mum would think of his behaviour).

And remember that scenes within sitcom or comedy drama can function like sketches. For instance, in a memorable transaction scene from *One Foot in the Grave*, it's set up that Victor has seen a card on the wall in Sainsbury's advertising a pair of black shoes for sale. When he goes to the address to buy them, the elderly vendor of the shoes explains they're brand new and belonged to her husband who has recently died. Victor sympathizes and she invites him to go through and try them on. Whereupon he discovers they are still on the feet of the deceased husband! The unreasonable shoe seller (entirely unaware there is anything inappropriate) proceeds to take them off her husband's lifeless feet as the appalled Victor looks on aghast.

In our improvisation, as in the above scenes, these are the two points of view (POV): the unreasonable point of view (the shop assistant) and the reasonable point of view (the customer). To improvise the scene:

- Two people will come up. One is the reasonable customer and one the unreasonable shop assistant. The kind of shop will be revealed right at the top of the improv by the customer. They will then say the *reasonable* thing they want.

- The shopkeeper then needs to unreasonably block them.

- From there, the game is for the reasonable customer to try every which way to get the shop assistant to see sense, but they will not budge.

- The scene will end with one person taking on the behaviour or perspective of the other.

In class, I tell the students that the improvised shop scene will begin with the person improvising the customer will set up what kind of shop it is in their opening line. For example, they might say, 'Wow, such a relief to find a pharmacy open at this hour.' Now the shop assistant (and the audience) know where we are and who's who. Let's say the customer next says he wants to buy condoms. It's good if there is some urgency to a scene, so the fact that they have established the hour is late and they are in a hurry to buy condoms allows us to imagine what's driving the purchase. It would be less engaging if the customer was merely buying condoms just to have them in stock in the hope of a future liaison. This is all set-up. The person playing the shop assistant (that we now know is a pharmacist) is aware the game is to unreasonably block the customer from getting what they want (in this case condoms), so let's imagine that in a moment of inspiration she explains to the customer that before he can buy the condoms, he needs to present his marriage certificate. That's the reveal. Now the absurdity needs to escalate, so when the stunned customer asks why, the pharmacist might say she is a person of strong traditional morals and as such does not want to be an accessory to sex outside wedlock. (Perhaps she could even tout her, as she sees it, broad-mindedness as she is quite happy if it's a same-sex marriage.) Let's see this in action. Here is a version of set-up/reveal for the scene that gets the essential idea across, though I feel at this point it's lacking something:

CUSTOMER: Wow, such a relief to find a pharmacy open at this hour.

PHARMACIST: Yes indeed. How can I help you?

CUSTOMER: Just a 48-pack of Cherry Lubricated Play Ultra-Thin condoms please, thanks.

PHARMACIST: Do you have your marriage certificate on you?

CUSTOMER: No, I do not!

PHARMACIST: Then you can't have them.

CUSTOMER: This is crazy – just sell me the condoms!

The sketch has only just begun here, so we can expect a couple more minutes of the customer trying and failing to buy condoms, but I feel this scene is getting off on the wrong footing. So, let's break off at this point and ask: how aware are your characters and do they care? The customer is aware there is a problem and cares. He *really* cares. He needs these condoms asap. Upping how much the voice-of-reason character cares tends to help the comedy of the scene. Now, how about the pharmacist? In the opening we've just seen, she is unaware her behaviour is unreasonable and so didn't care about the customer's reactions. But how about if it was less cut and dry? Let's ratchet up the awareness of the pharmacist a few notches. Not enough to realize that her whole outlook is absurd, but enough to know that it's a little delicate, and for her to care a little more about the customer, even though, ultimately, she won't give him what he wants.

Then on the customer's side, yes, he is aware and he does care, but I didn't buy his reactions in the above version. It didn't ring true. If this kind of performance was given in class, I'd rewind them and get them to go again, thinking about how *they* would react in this situation. It's natural to focus on the 'funny' unreasonable character in the scene, but they are only as funny as the reactions they are getting from the reasonable character. So, the more attention you put on them, and the more seriously you take their journey through the scene, the funnier it will be. Here is a version of the scene where I feel the reasonable character is more plausibly adjusting and reacting to this unexpected situation and the pharmacist has their awareness/caring level tweaked up a couple of notches:

CUSTOMER: Wow, such a relief to find a pharmacy open at this hour.

PHARMACIST: Yes indeed. How can I help you?

CUSTOMER: Just a 48-pack of Cherry Lubricated Play Ultra-Thin condoms please, thanks.

PHARMACIST: Condoms? Er . . . oh dear, we seem to be sold out.

CUSTOMER: Um . . . I'm sorry . . . but I can see some right behind you?

PHARMACIST: What? [TURNS ROUND] Oh yes! Yes, that's right. We do have some.

CUSTOMER: Great.

PHARMACIST: Just one quick thing.

CUSTOMER: Yes?

PHARMACIST: Er . . . Do you have your marriage certificate on you?

CUSTOMER: Do I . . . *what?*

PHARMACIST: Sorry, it's just I do need to see a marriage certificate.

CUSTOMER: You're joking?

PHARMACIST: Not at all. I'm sorry, I know it's a hassle, but as I'm sure you can appreciate as a person of traditional moral values, I don't want to be an accessory to an act of, ahem, love-making out of wedlock. So, if I could just see your marriage certificate, we can complete the transaction.

CUSTOMER: I don't believe this!

PHARMACIST: I'm very broad-minded. It can be a same-sex marriage certificate.

CUSTOMER: Now look, I don't have a marriage certificate for the simple reason that I'm not married. And even if I were, I wouldn't be carrying it around with me in order to prove my status whenever I want to buy condoms!

PHARMACIST: Then I'm afraid I can't sell them to you.

CUSTOMER: What? Right, I want to speak to the manager.

PHARMACIST: Sir, I *am* the manager . . .

. . . and so on, playing the game of the customer trying different ways round the immoveable obstacle. How does this version read to you? I prefer it to the previous iteration. I feel that ratcheting the awareness and caring of the pharmacist up a touch, alongside the customer reacting more naturally, creates more textured and believable action. Now I feel we can buy into the characters' journeys through the scene. By the way. I went for a very specific (albeit made up) brand of condoms here, the 'Cherry Lubricated Play Ultra-Thin' condoms. Being specific is stronger than just saying 'I want to buy some condoms'. (And I made it a 48-pack to hint at the customer's sexual exuberance.) Which brings us to the payoff. Usually when people are improvising the scene, if they haven't reached the end themselves in two to three minutes, I'll call out that in the next thirty seconds they need to end it. The instruction is for one character to take the perspective of the other. One way is for the unreasonable character to suddenly see sense and take the reasonable perspective – which can be done in a funny way, especially if when having done so, they flip straight back to being unreasonable. For example:

PHARMACIST: Okay, okay. I guess you're right. It is the twenty-first century. It is a bit much to insist on a wedding certificate before I'll sell you condoms.

CUSTOMER: Thank you.

PHARMACIST: No, an engagement ring will do just fine.

This is what I call a 'false dawn' ending (see Chapter 5), where it looks for a moment like everything is resolved – and then it isn't. The other way round is perhaps more common: the reasonable character buys into the perspective of the unreasonable one. In our pharmacist example the customer might go 'Okay, okay. I'll just go and get a quickie wedding and I'll be back.' Then perhaps the pharmacist could add, 'No need to go anywhere sir. Just call your date to come and join us. We conduct marriages here on the premises.' In which case we now get a closing revelation that changes our perspective on everything that has come before. It now seems like the pharmacist was angling to up-sell to their in-house wedding service.

Our pharmacist scene could be a sketch, or it could be scene within a longer narrative. Having got a clear picture of how they behave in one situation, then you can ask: how would that person behave in other contexts given what we've learned about them? When we spoke, improviser Katy Schutte imagined how our pharmacist might develop as a character beyond the pharmacy. She says of her behaviour:

> She believes she's helping the customer not do something bad in their life. If she's like that about condoms, what's she like in other situations? What food would she bring to a party? She'll probably bring celery because it's neutral and it's not going to offend anyone and it's good for you. So, she tries to look after everyone and it's a mothering thing. Or if it's a control thing, you could go a different way. She comes to a party with a board game that everyone has to play with a lot of very elaborate rules. You ask: if this is true, what else is? Where can I take that person? They're fun to play with, what else do they do?

After we've played it with a reasonable customer and an unreasonable shop assistant (in different shops) a few times, we'll then play it the other way round, where the shop assistant has the reasonable point of view and the customer has the unreasonable perspective. So, this time the customer wants something *unreasonable* and is being *reasonably* blocked by the shop assistant. As a sketch example of this reversed dynamic, we might consider a Key & Peele sketch where the reasonable shopkeeper in a bed retailer has to deal with the bizarre antics of the customer who wants to try out the beds by jumping on them and lying on his back, bouncing up and down violently while enacting a bizarre sexual situation, which he clearly believes is entirely reasonable behaviour. Key's reactions as the shop assistant are a masterclass in voice-of-reason reactions. The sketch also a has a big surprise at the end which I won't give away here.

In the bookshop sketch from the *Monty Python's Contractual Obligations Album* (originally a pre-Python sketch), John Cleese's reasonable bookseller is faced with Graham Chapman's unreasonable customer who wants to buy a series of books that don't exist and real books whose titles have been distorted ('A Sale of Two Titties'), authors' names distorted ('Charles Dikkens the well-known Dutch author'), and a non-existent edition of a real book ('Olsen's Standard Book of British Birds', 'the one without the gannet in it'). This sketch is another good one for illustrating the journey of the reasonable character. Cleese's voice-of-reason shopkeeper goes on an emotional journey: helpful, confused, annoyed, dismissive, angry, manic and finally when he catches the customer out when he names an apparently absurd book that he actually does have in the shop – 'Ethel the Aardvark Goes Quantity Surveying' – determined to win. The sketch ends with the bookseller triumphantly finding the book but the customer revealing that he doesn't have any money to pay for it. Determined to make him have the book, the bookseller buys it for the customer. At which point he reveals he can't read. So, the bookseller has to read it to him. It's a role reversal ending with the bookseller effectively stepping into the role of the customer, paying for and reading the book.

When I ask the students to improvise a shop scene from this perspective, it's the reasonable shopkeeper who reveals the type of shop at the top of the scene and it's up to the customer, at some point in the opening exchanges, to reveal the unreasonable thing they want. To give them a steer, I suggest it might be a product that doesn't exist. It could, for example, be someone wanting to buy a Samsung Seance Phone, believing they can message their deceased relatives. Or if it is a real product, then they might have unreasonable expectations of it, for instance believing that a fragrance will make them instantly and irresistibly attractive to all members of the opposite sex and being annoyed when the shopkeeper doesn't instantly fall for them when they spray a bit on their wrist. It really can be anything, no matter how outlandish, as long as the performers play a believable journey through the scene. The fun of the dynamic is that the shopkeeper is instructed to stay professional and as patient and polite as they can (although this will be severely tested) while trying to make the customer see sense. (If you've ever worked in a shop, you'll recognize this dynamic when faced with a challenging customer.)

Once you've finished with shops and other service contexts, you can move on to other situations. The scene can be about anything and the same dynamic is in play. Shorn of the transaction context, it's essentially:

1   Character A wants something reasonable and is being unreasonably blocked by Character B.

2   Character A wants something unreasonable and is being reasonably blocked by Character B.

You might have the reasonable person wanting directions in the street and the unreasonable person not giving them, or giving clearly incorrect directions. Or it might be a date scene in a restaurant and the unreasonable person proposes marriage straight after the starter. Or it might be a TV interview where the unreasonable interviewer will only ask questions about the celebrity's toenails.

Whatever the scenario you come up with, as you play the game (and you might alternatively be playing the game as a writer at your laptop), the scene will stay on track if:

1   The unreasonable character sticks with their unreasonable perspective and doesn't deviate from it.

2   The reasonable character tries lots of different ways to get round the obstruction – but all to no avail. In class, the reasonable person will often

get stuck in a groove of doing one thing to try to get what they want. For example, they keep shouting at the unreasonable person. What gives the scene, and your character, life and movement is if you try different ways to solve the problem. You might go from reasoning to flattery to bribery to threats . . .

3 The unreasonable character stays emotionally fairly neutral – after all, in their mind they are the reasonable one! – while the reasonable person goes on an escalating emotional journey.

And problems that can derail it include:

4 You start bringing in other games that are so big they take over the original idea. When the students are improvising the scene, I will jump in and get it back on track if one of them brings in an entirely new, big idea. You only need one idea for a sketch or a funny scene! From a writing point of view, a takeaway here is not to panic and overcomplicate or bring in more and more elements in an effort to make it funny. Just truthfully play the game.

5 In the search for laughs, the reasonable behaviour person starts going along with the unreasonable one (this could happen right at the end but not in the body of the scene). If the reasonable character starts to adopt the strangeness of the other character, I'll stop a scene and reset the voice-of-reason's behaviour. Yes, it might get laughs, but the overall funniness of the scene is best served by the normal behaviour staying that way: a big part of the funniness is watching them struggle. The beauty of it is that often in class, a student playing the voice-of-reason will stop and say, 'This is really hard, I don't know what to say.' Well, that is exactly where the character is at, so if you're feeling that way, stay in the scene and play that!

6 The unreasonable person gives in and starts being reasonable. Will Hines remarks, 'I have to make that point if I'm teaching in a class and, just by coincidence, a more confident, capable actor is playing the voice-of-reason and a newer, less competent person is playing the unusual one. In this situation the unusual one sometimes gives up. I'll have to say, "Don't let this person's confidence turn you off. Your job is to stay with your point of view." You have to be careful: you can't let the voice-of-reason win. They may have the more sensible hand but they still can't win. They have to lose.' In the Parrot sketch, John Cleese's customer can't get Michael Palin's pet shop owner to give in and acknowledge that the parrot is dead. So, whether you're writing a script or improvising a scene, you have to have a laser-like focus on the points of view of the characters and keep them working to get what they want, without either side ever winning.

And finally, you can play option 3! Which is the single point-of-view weird world option where both characters play the scene out *as if* the strange thing is entirely normal. Returning to our pharmacy scene, and the idea of the pharmacist wanting to see a marriage certificate before selling the man condoms, if it were a weird world single point-of-view sketch then the man would accept this as a requirement. If he just produced the certificate it'd be game over, so maybe he has a fake marriage certificate that the pharmacist is sceptical about. Then the whole scene could be played *as if* it's someone underage trying to buy alcohol. It's always worth considering if any particular comic idea would be funnier as a 2 x POV normal world or a 1 x POV weird world scenario. You could even try it both ways and see which is funnier. Then the character's intellectual and emotional points of view will add individuality to their characterization.

Scenes and characters in stand-up

Sketches are typically in one location and unfold in real time across a few minutes with a small number of characters and play one clear game, but as we've seen, stand-ups can take a number of angles, playing several games on one topic, and they can also freely move backwards and forwards in time. For instance, continuing with transaction scenes, Jerry Seinfeld's supermarket bit is punctuated by a whole series of act-outs, essentially micro-sketches, exploring different aspects of the shopping experience. The first act-out is of a supermarket shopper marching purposefully into the store to make their purchases, and once inside they find themselves in a retail trance wandering zombie-like around the store, hypnotized by the place. He later on goes on to portray people in the supermarket who are unsure if they need milk, and then people who have bought too much milk and, in a race against the expiration dates, are having huge bowls of cereal, washing their face with milk and offering it to the neighbourhood cats. Seinfeld, as is typical with his observational approach, is more of a spectator than a player. In Bill Burr's take on grocery stores, he too drops into a sequence of act-outs, but he is at the heart of the action, beginning with finding himself at a self-service checkout and sarcastically saying he thought he was a comedian but now he finds he works at a grocery store. Next, he goes back in time to the inception of the idea and a gruff Italian American grocer telling his customers to do the work themselves and then he jumps forward in time to when such checkouts are universal, at which time, he says, he will no longer pay for anything. He acts out rolling hams out of the store's doors to waiting friends outside. The great advantage for the solo stand-up performer is this ability to jump immediately in and out of scenes and instantly shift time or location, as well has having an ongoing commentary on your thoughts and views of the situation.

When I'm thinking about the persona of a stand-up comic, I'll also sometimes ask: are you a Straight Line or Wavy Line comic? I'd say Burr is Straight Line, steaming ahead with his uncompromising attitude, while Seinfeld is Wavy Line as he struggles to understand the foibles of modern behaviour. When we spoke, I told Steve Kaplan how I use his Straight Line–Wavy Line model in stand-up. He says, 'Certainly Straight Line, Wavy Line works in stand-up. It's not as clear as in a sketch, but as a stand-up you're either letting the audience observe you or you're observing them.' If you're letting the audience observe you, then you're the one behaving bizarrely, ridiculously or unreasonably and everyone else has to deal with you: you're a Straight Line comic. You're just marching ahead with your odd perspective and we all have to deal with it. On the other hand, if you're observing the world, being affected emotionally, struggling to understand, then you're the Wavy Line. Part of the pleasure of Seinfeld is that *he* feels people are behaving unreasonably but *they* are not aware of doing so, until he (caring) points it out. Burr, on the other hand, will often behave unreasonably himself, be aware of it and not care. As a stand-up you can also be comically unaware of how you are coming across. Steve Kaplan suggested an example: 'Like early Howie Mandel, who would do something silly and then say, "What? What?" like he didn't know what happened.' From Toronto, Canada, Mandel would come out laughing manically with a bizarre outfit and odd prop gags, like having a bird attached to a baseball cap and saying 'A shit flew over and birded on my hat' (a reversal – see the next chapter). He'd react to the audience laughter like he had no idea what was funny: 'What? What?' Here he is playing a lack of self-awareness and it's dramatic irony – we the audience get something he doesn't. When you're playing with dramatic irony, your imperfections should be crystal clear to the audience but not to you. You are as blissfully unaware of how you are coming across as is the waiter at the Burgundy Loaf. So, how self-aware are you as a stand-up and how much do you care?

At the time of writing, I've just been working with a newer stand-up who has a liking for saying dark or outrageous things to the audience to get a reaction (a not uncommon strategy among newer comics). He recognized that this had a limited shelf life but wasn't sure what to do about it. For instance, he has a well-crafted if dark joke about a murder on the estate where he used to live. It was a misdirection joke, in that he makes the audience think he was relieved to move away as he might have been the victim, but then they discover he actually meant he might have been the murderer. Rather than simply saying this joke to the audience, I suggested he put it into a context, into a story. In my version, he tells the audience that he's recently moved into a nicer area and that he's met his new neighbour – and he could be pleased that he's actually talking to his neighbour in the anonymous big city. He then acts out the conversation they had when they met. They talk about his old area and she says she heard about the murder on the news. Then he says *to her* that he's pleased he got away because it could have been him . . . committing the murder. She reacts, appalled. I suggested he say to the audience, '*I* thought it was funny but she looked like she was thinking, "I must put five more locks on my front door."' Then he could add, 'We haven't spoken since.' What I've done here is take the original joke, put it into a context and introduced a reacting character who the audience can relate to. It also introduces awareness on his part about how the joke makes him look and he cares about the reaction he's getting as it is affecting his relationship with his neighbour. It makes it all a lot richer than just saying the line to shock the audience.

Caring about his relationship with his neighbour gives this stand-up a warmer persona than the original shock approach. And as a writer of scripts, how you feel about your characters will affect the tone of the piece. At one extreme you might think your characters are awful human beings and enjoy inflicting indignities on them. This tends to result in a cooler, even a harsh tone. In contrast, you might feel great affection for your characters, which will result in a far warmer show where the audience care about the characters and can come to love them as you do. Finding an emotional connection to your characters, actually caring about them, can take your work to another level of audience engagement, whether you're inspired by a true story like the *Shrill* series or are writing a 'what if' concept like the 'Last Fuckable Day' sketch. On which subject, asking 'What if things were different?' and creating alternative realities is a device we go on to consider in depth in the next chapter.

Chapter 7

'What If?' in Online Comedy and Beyond

In a Laugh Factory set that's on YouTube, Camilla Cleese talks about her dysfunctional relationship with her mobile phone, saying there should be an app that texts you when the traffic lights go green as she's fed up with being honked by the car behind. Cleese says that Siri is basically her best friend, then she goes on to explore the question *what if* Siri were a guy instead of a girl? What if Siri were Simon? She then goes on to imagine that you'd ask (brightly) 'Hey Simon, what's the weather like outside?' and he'd reply (dumbly) '*Huh?*' This is followed by a series of questions you might ask Siri being responded to by 'Simon', who, incongruously for a high-tech digital assistant, answers like a dumb boyfriend. In this chapter I'll look at these kinds of 'what if?' comedy concepts. We'll look at lots of online examples and I also take the opportunity to speak to some terrific online comedy-makers about their work and how they've progressed in comedy with the internet as a platform.

Turning to sketch comedy, I searched for videos on YouTube with the words 'What if comedy' and the top result was the sketch 'If Gandhi Took a Yoga Class'. This great CollegeHumor sketch does exactly what the title promises. Gandhi has been put into a modern yoga class where his 'woke' mat mates are bemused by his authentic Hindu yogic ways and patronize him mercilessly, while he is equally puzzled by the strange turn this ancient Indian discipline has taken. The second video had the title 'What if James Bond was Australian?' You can already imagine how this sketch might play out. Online sketches do tend to flag up the game in the title, so that you'll want to click on it. This does encourage this kind of 'what if?' thinking because these ideas can be summed up in an eye-catching sentence that makes for good click bait, like 'If Siri was a Dude'.

'What if?' in improv and writing

To explore 'what if?', here's an exercise that you can do as a writer, working through different angles on a subject. It can also be played out as an improv exercise where you work through a series of different variations on one premise. Any starting point will do, but I'm going to choose a high-stakes situation, as when there is more at stake any absurdity is naturally heightened. Let's say our situation is a pair of criminals planning a bank raid. To begin with, as improvisers, you might play it once straight. Resist trying to find the funny in this. This is about establishing how the scene would normally play out. Writers could go online and find (dramatic) examples of such scenes on YouTube. Once you've established the baseline reality, the challenge now is changing key variables to produce a series of different comic versions of the scene. Note that the situation is reset every time. You don't carry over any of the changes from the previous version. All of these will be 'weird world' sketches, in that there isn't a voice-of-reason questioning what's happening. When you make each change, you're aiming to keep everything else right about the scene – in terms of energy, tone and emotion – whilst changing the one key detail. Here are the changes with a bank robber example for each.

Unsaid said

The game is to have the characters talk openly about a subtext or hidden agenda that normally wouldn't be voiced.

Our bank robbers talk about being emasculated as men having lost their jobs and needing to prove their virility with a violent raid, alongside gaining some status-enhancing riches to compensate for their erectile dysfunction.

Change WHY

This game is changing the motive for the characters' action.

Rather than stealing the money to fund their lavish lifestyles or criminal schemes, the robbers want funds to add to their collection of My Little Ponies.

Change WHEN

Change the time period the action happens in, or bring in a character from another era.

Our bank robbers are now in Turkey in 600 BC and planning on mounting the first ever currency robbery on the coins minted by King Alyattes.

Change WHERE

Relocate the action.

Instead of the planning for a bank raid taking place in some dodgy East End boozer, our robbers are planning the raid in the queue at the bank itself, with all the attendant awkwardness this introduces.

Change WHO

Now the game is changing who the characters are.

The robbers are two nuns planning the bank raid. Or it might be Sir Patrick Stewart and Sir Ian McKellen. Basically, anyone unlikely to be robbing a bank.

Change WHAT

Now the game is changing the subject or the object of the scenario.

The robbers are planning on stealing all of the bank's pens on chains.

Change HOW

The game is changing the method your characters are using to achieve their goal.

The robbers decide to tickle the money out of the bank staff.

Reverse it

In this game you switch round the dynamic.

So now it's bank tellers planning on stealing money from villains, maybe feeling they don't get paid enough.

Rescale it

Change the size of some element of the situation, either growing or shrinking it.

Now our robbers are planning on raiding a piggy bank.

Personify

Give something non-human a voice, character and attitudes.

Our robbers now become jackdaws who are planning on stealing the nuts from a squirrel. Or, if they were to become 'things', they could be phones with 1% battery life planning a raid on a portable power bank.

As you work through each angle on an idea, some won't go anywhere, some will feel like one-liners but some will gain traction and will merit working on. The high-stakes scene is a good starting-point, but you can use any kind of initial situation and it's also a particularly good exercise for parodies. Pick a TV show, media format or a movie and work through each of the changes in turn. For example, in a pleasing *change who*, *That Mitchell & Webb Sound* had a great radio sketch that's a charity appeal where they take Médecins Sans Frontières and make it Hairdressers Sans Frontières, who take their styling skills into disaster zones.

Unsaid said

Let's now work through each of these changes in more detail. Firstly, *what if* someone actually spoke the truth of a situation? We saw an example in Chapter 2, where Peter Cook has the prime minister of the day actually voicing criticisms of himself. Or another sketch from *That Mitchell & Webb Sound* has a couple who have written their own wedding vows saying things like 'Normally I wouldn't go for someone like you, but let's face it I'm not getting any younger so I've decided to settle.' In both cases what is 'unsaid' is now being 'said'. In a stand-up routine about weddings, Jim Gaffigan has the couple speaking the absurd subtext (as he sees it) to the whole premise of a wedding. They say, proudly, that thanks to the wedding they can start their married life with a total fantasy before going on a completely unjustified vacation.

There's a great sketch example of this kind of *unsaid said* game in Key & Peele's school bully sketch. In the *set-up*, a school kid (Key) is sitting on the steps of a school, the school bell ringing and a group of other kids leaving the school behind him. The school bully (Peele) breaks away from group and, looming over the reading boy, knocks the book out of his hand and asks, 'Why are you reading bitch?' as his friends smile with approval in the background. The boy asks 'Why you gotta bother me man?' To which the bully replies, in the *reveal*, 'Because . . . I'm not doing very well at school. I'm reading at a third-grade level, I really don't want to get left back, so when I see someone reading for fun it makes me feel that much more stupid, and then I get mad.' The game here is firstly that he is speaking the subtext – it's an unsaid said – and that he incongruously says it with energy and venom as if he's made a bullying comment.

The sketch escalates with the bully alternating between moments of aggression and aggressive self-revelation. The *payoff* introduces a new character when the father of the bully shows up in his pickup truck to collect him from school. Here it's a 'peas-in-a-pod' gag, where the father behaves exactly like this son. He says he's going to 'beat on' his son because the boy's mother left him and he needs to block out the guilt he feels for mistreating the boy. Then the bully explains to his victim that he is going to internalize that and unknowingly transfer it to him tomorrow.

Change WHY

Changing *why* characters are doing something is an approach that has paid off for writer, actor, filmmaker and character comic Steve Whiteley. Steve and I have worked together for a number of years, with me acting as sounding board, script editor and live director, a collaboration that began when I directed the Edinburgh shows of his spoof urban poet character Wisebowm, which has gone on to be a BBC Radio 4 show which I helped develop and script-edited. While all this was happening, Steve came to me with an idea he'd had for a short film that he'd write, direct and star in. At the time there was an epidemic of crime in London carried out by young men riding mopeds. In particular, people were having mobile phones swiped out of their hands. Steve's idea was this: what if the thieves were actually stealing them to get people off their phones so they can become more aware of the present moment? So instead of doing it to make money, they're doing it in an aggressively altruistic act to spread mindfulness. We developed the idea together and this became the short film *Swiped* (2019).

Steve released *Swiped* both online and into film festivals. As Steve recalls, 'I could have released it on my own YouTube channel but because I hadn't been releasing anything for ages, there was no engaged audience there. The last thing I wanted was to spend time and money making it, only for it to fall flat online. So instead I partnered up with the YouTube channel Million Youth Media. They promote and release filmmakers' short films on their channel. They've usually got an urban theme to them and they have a huge built-in audience, with over 300,000 subscribers. They are very particular about what they accept and fortunately they liked *Swiped* and released it.' Our intention was for the short to act as a taster for a sitcom, and having it do well online would make it a more compelling pitch. Steve continues, 'Luckily it went viral on YouTube and via snippets on social media. And then at the same time, I was working with a company called Festival Formula who put together a strategy for entering it into film festivals. They suggest the ones the film would be suitable for, because there's hundreds of festivals and you can waste lots of money entering the wrong ones. It got into some really well-regarded festivals including Palm Springs Short Fest, which is the biggest short film festival in the US.' Steve went out there and made lots of contacts and as a result he told me, 'I got offered a role in a sitcom pilot for Baby Cow having met the director at the Palm Springs festival and staying in touch. That's just an example of all the ricochet effects that can happen just by getting out there.'

Change WHERE

The first *Monty Python* sketch I ever saw was one I stumbled upon while changing channels as a teenager. At the time I had no idea of *Flying Circus* and was brilliantly bemused by turning over to discover there was a programme named 'Storage Jars' that rather than taking place in a TV studio was instead happening outdoors in a war zone where the presenter, who I now know to be Terry Jones, is valiantly talking about the merits and uses of storage jars while bombs are going off all around him; so changing *where* something takes place.

Dan Audritt and Kat Butterworth's Comedy Central online sketch series *Modern Horror Stories* has many 'what if?' sketches. (I directed Dan in his stand-up hour *Better Man*, which I talk about in Chapter 3.) First up, I picked a 'change where' sketch from the series which relocates where a meeting takes place. Dan told me, 'Meeting your partner's parents for the first time is a modern-day horror feeling because you feel so judged, so what's the ultimate feeling of being judged? Then we thought about [the dog show] Crufts where they're literally judging something, so then we made it Boyfriend Crufts.' In the sketch the girlfriend is bringing her partner to meet her parents and they are judging him in a dog show type context. Kat says, 'We hired a really good art director and said, "You only have this budget so you have to think very creatively about how to stretch it."' This led to them replicating the environment of Crufts on a bowling green. Dan recalls, 'It was hilarious artwork.'

Dan and Kat worked on *Modern Horror Stories* with Jon Aird, a producer who works across online, social media and television with an interest in finding and nurturing talent. Dan told me he'd met Jon while he was studying at the NFTS (National Film and Theatre School) when Jon came in to do a talk about online comedy. Having kept in touch while making his first online videos and developing his stand-up, Dan was eventually hired by Jon as an assistant producer making online comedy. Kat had done the same course at the NFTS and she too contacted Jon to, as she put it, 'pester him a lot to see if there was anything that I could get involved in'. Jon introduced Dan and Kat. As Dan recalls, 'So I sketched something out and then sent it to Kat and she tore it apart.' Kat responded with relish, 'Yes, I tore it apart!' Dan went on, 'Then we met up, you told me your ideas for it and instead of me redrafting it, I just said, "Do you just want to write it with me?" and we've been writing together ever since and it's become a team of three: Kat, me and Jon.'

After writing some online sketches for Comic Relief, Jon gave them the challenge of coming up with 'a viral', and as it was around Halloween, he wanted a horror theme. Dan notes, 'We came up with the idea of 'Modern Day Horrors'. Kat had the idea of it being about dating.' Kat adds, 'It then became about a girl who starts dating a guy, realized he isn't on social media, freaks out, then it plays out as a horror trailer parody.' Dan continues, 'We put it out online and thought nothing more of it. It has about 250 million views now. Comedy Central liked the modern horrors angle and they commissioned us for an online series, *Modern Horror Stories*. As it was online the budget was pretty low.' Kat adds, 'But we'd made YouTube videos, so we knew how to make stuff cheaply, so we felt quite confident we could do it.' Dan elaborated that 'Everything was made by the two of us and then when we went into the edit, we had an editor, but we were in there every day.' Kat remembers, 'It was a lot of work and lot of late nights and weekends. Basically, we lived at Comedy Central for a few months.' So fittingly they *changed where* they were residing!

Many online sketches take the internet itself as a subject, and in terms of 'change where' a fun game to play is to take something from the internet and ask *what if* it played out in the real, offline world. This has become a staple of online comedy, with a recent example from BBC Wales, *If High Street Shopping was like Online Shopping*, quickly going viral on a number of platforms, receiving 15 million views on Facebook in under a fortnight. The granddaddy of all these online-in-the-real-world sketches must be *A Conference Call in Real Life*. Made by Tripp & Tyler in 2014, at the time of writing it has 17 million views on YouTube. I asked Tripp Crosby what led up to this breakthrough video and he told me, 'We had been making funny sketch comedy for six or seven years at that point. We had just been creating comedy sketches over and over, many of them were not good – in fact, some of them were horrible – but over time, in comedy, you learn an instinct.' At the outset they didn't have any particular goal:

We started out just by creating whatever we wanted and putting it on our YouTube channel. Fortunately, we got in really early with YouTube and built an audience really fast, which gave us enough exposure to start doing corporate video. We did *A Conference Call in Real Life* because we thought it was a funny idea, but we ended up striking a nerve with every industry because everyone is feeling those same pain points. We accidentally made the perfect video to bring in brand work. We had this long line of people wanting us to make videos for them. It was a happy accident.

Change WHEN

In another *Modern Horror Stories* sketch, Dan and Kat change *when* something happened. Kat explains, 'We asked ourselves if our grandparents had met *today*, what kind of stories would they have? Then we came up with the sketch that's a lot of old couples telling how they met and they are all quite disgusting stories of meeting on Tinder or Grindr. We thought about having the cast made to look old, but we thought, no, we want to be authentic old people!'

In another 'change when', a *Mitchell & Webb* sketch takes a modern day TV gameshow format and transports it into the future in the shape of 'Remain Indoors', a tragic post-apocalyptic show on the 'British Emergency Broadcasting System' where survivors of 'the event' take part in the ramshackle quiz and try to suppress their traumatic memories while the viewers are regularly exhorted to remain indoors. (Rewatching the sketches at the height of the Covid-19 lockdown made them feel suddenly prophetic.) So, they've taken a banal TV format and relocated it from a contemporary TV studio to a post-apocalyptic realm.

Conversely a lot of comedies set in history have anachronistic jokes where modern day things play out in the past or where historical people have knowledge they couldn't possibly have had. For example, Palin and Jones's (pre-*Python*) *The Complete and Utter History of Britain* had an estate agent showing a Neolithic couple around Stonehenge as if it were a property they are interested in buying, or Eddie Izzard imagining the pagan builders of the henge complaining about their lot and wishing the Christians would hurry up and get there.

Change WHO

Steve Whiteley had a hit online sketch in 2014 with *If Men Had Periods*. This particular *change who* has been mined by everyone from Gloria Steinem to Ben Elton to Michelle Wolf. Steve's angle was to have men act *as if* they were women on their periods, with the aim of capturing the truth of women's behaviour but transposing it to men. He told me:

> That sketch goes back to when I was making the first series of sketches for my YouTube channel. That could have been quite a divisive topic. I wanted to make sure that even though we were really mocking men, with the idea that men couldn't deal with what women go through on a monthly basis, I wanted to make sure that the behaviour and emotional aspects were representative of women's actual experience. So, I spoke to some female comedians that I knew and said, 'Look, this is the script we would love your thoughts [about]. Is this real? Is this believable?' I think that really helped get it to a place where it connected with people. When it went viral, I could see why it did because women could relate to it and it was taking the piss out of men as well.

In a spoof *change who* example entitled *Future Female Film Reboots*, sketch trio Muriel take the trend for remaking male-led films with female stars and take it to an absurd degree, with the likes of Emma Thompson as the Godfather, and Jennifer Lawrence as Rocky. (Muriel are made up of Janine Horouni,

Sally O'Reilly and Meg Salter, and I speak with Meg below when we come to reversal and then personification.) And at the time of writing, improviser Katy Schutte is working on a web series that changes who we're focusing on in a narrative. She told me, 'I have written and it'll be filming soon, a web series where each episode is a different trope of romcoms but we're following the side characters, like the best friends, instead of the leads. The action is adjacent to the romcom.' This inspired change of focus is reminiscent of Tom Stoppard's *Rosencrantz and Guildenstern Are Dead* where, instead of Hamlet, we follow the titular pair of minor characters who intermittently come in and out of the action of the original play.

Change WHAT

Having begun with sketches online, Steve Whiteley was introduced to Dave Tozer, who was making comedy music videos on his YouTube channel, and in 2015 they made a track where Steve was rapping about going 'Gluten Free', changing *what* a rapper would be rhyming about. Like Tripp & Tyler, Steve also monetized his work by moving into making comedy videos for big brands, eventually establishing his comedy content company Offkey World. Steve elaborates, 'For Paperchase we made a funny video with all these hard men creating homemade Mother's Day cards for their mums (changing *what* they would more stereotypically be doing). That won a Young Director of the Year Award at Cannes Lions, the advertising festival.' At one point, Steve made a comedy music video for an Asian shaving brand: 'I co-wrote the lyrics, and I went into the studio and made the music with a producer. They loved it and it went viral. That director ended up becoming creative director of BuzzFeed. I was fortunate that all of the sketches I'd done, like *If Men Had Periods*, were a very BuzzFeed type of content. It fitted into their aesthetic and their humour and before I knew it I was producing two or three videos a month for them. I saved a lot of that money from BuzzFeed and then I reinvested that into the production of *Swiped* [see 'Change WHY' above].'

Speaking of corporations, in a great online sketch, *The Expert: 7 Red Lines*, by Lauris Beinerts, an engineer is being briefed on a task in a corporate meeting where *what* is being talked about has been changed from a technical issue to the apparently simple matter of drawing a series of red lines. However, the entire situation is played out *as if* they are still talking about something highly specialized and the corporate people are way out of their depth, asking meaningless questions like 'Can you use green ink to draw the red lines?' The sketch hilariously captures the dilemma of experts having to deal with the uninformed questions of lay people and, with over 24 million views, has clearly struck a chord.

Reverse it

One of my favourite of Muriel's sketches, *Witch Hunt*, is a reversal. Inspired by the ubiquity of that phrase where men in particular claim they are a victim of an orchestrated 'witch hunt', they brainstormed a comic angle on it. When we spoke, Meg Salter recalled, 'We must have sat around for a few hours trying to work out what the flip was. That was the one that took longest, but we were so happy when it came out.' The game of the sketch is to take the idea of a witch hunt literally and whereas in a historical witch hunt it'd primarily be men who were afraid women were witches, they flipped it to be contemporary women who are afraid that men are witches. Meg said the evidence was, 'their haircuts only cost £12 and they can wee standing up'. It's also an example of playing with time periods, as later in the sketch they are dressed as seventeenth-century puritanical witch hunters with pitchforks interrogating a terrified corporate man in an underground car park. (The previously discussed *If Men Had Periods* is also of course a reversal of the normal situation.)

Rescale it

Wild-haired, deeply deadpan stand-up Steven Wright often works with changes of scale. In one classic 'scaling-down' gag, he talks about how he was a ticket tout scalping tickets for the deli. He says he sold a number 3 for 28 bucks. In a memorable scaling up joke, Wright says he has a map of the United States where the scale is 1 mile = 1 mile. He says he spent the summer folding it up. And in an online UCB sketch (which doubtless originated in improvisation), the BP Deepwater Horizon oil spill of 2010 is reduced to the scale of a BP executive spilling coffee in a meeting. Their hapless attempts to deal with the spill parody their real-life attempts to deal with the oil spill (garnering them over 13 million views). For another online example of scaling down, Kat suggested, 'Not being able to afford a house is a big millennial problem at the moment. So [on *Modern Horror Stories*] we make it Millennialopoly, a Monopoly-like board game where you can't afford to buy houses.'

In a scaling-up *Modern Horror Stories* sketch, they scale targeted ads up from personal screen size to billboard size, where every billboard is running very personal targeted ads for each individual walking past. The producers queried how realistic it would be to actually realize this idea on their budget, but as Dan said, 'We've just done so many cheap things we know what's possible. We know that to change a billboard costs thousands of pounds, but to get someone to do it in post, as long as they're shot it in a certain way, we could get them for two days and it can be done.'

Personification

Personification is when something non-human is given a speaking voice, an attitude and a character. In stand-up, for example, in one of Eddie Izzard's most beloved routines, he observes that fruit seems to become over-ripe when your back is turned. Then he anthropomorphizes fruit in a bowl waiting until you leave the room, when they go 'Ripen now!' Radio too is a great medium for personification, as, like stand-up, there is no need for set or costume. For example, Mitchell & Webb have an incompetent shower temperature dial and shower head who agree between themselves that because a man trying to have a shower has the temperature dial halfway, that must mean he wants it scorching half the time and ice cold the other half. Then there's wonderful sketch group Cowards who in their radio show personify coins in a wishing well where a pompous guinea patronizes modern coins. In Muriel's breakthrough online sketch *If Tube Lines Were People*, they play the personification of various tube lines, for example, the aged District and Bakerloo lines are doddery pensioners.

Meg told me, 'Again with that one we had a general idea and things to say, and we improvised around that. We uploaded that and it just went mad. It went viral very quickly and soon publications were talking about it.' Media coverage included the *London Evening Standard*. 'As a result Suzy Grant from the BBC, who we're now working with, got in touch.' I asked Meg the million-dollar question: what makes something go viral? Aside from luck, she said she felt the things that go viral are often on divisive topics that stir up strong opinions on either side of the argument.

Finally, I asked how Muriel got together and Meg told me, 'Me, Janine and Sally had all gone to LAMDA [London Academy of Music and Dramatic Art] together. We did the two-year course. It was very hard, as they tell you, but no one really believes it. Not enough roles were coming our way, so we decided we'd do something together.' They started off making short online comedy dating videos (doubtless inspired by the brilliant *Smack the Pony* ones) that reached a select but appreciative audience online. As Meg remarks, 'Those were our very first things, because it was really easy to do. We could film them on our phones or iPads. We'd have some costume and a starting-point then we'd improvise and we'd do a jump-cut edit. It meant that we could just improvise around the subject and cut it together later. They got a bigger response than we thought they would.' I asked Meg how improvised their work is these days. She told me, 'When we first started it was all improvised. Whereas as soon as we got more people on board, and time became more precious, we had to be more disciplined. Before we just improvised around an idea, whereas now it is scripted. But on the day, we always play around a little, or we'll write a line and have a few alternatives to try. So, we still leave it a little loose.'

Inspired by the success of their dating videos, Muriel decided to film a sketch with improved production values, getting friends on board to help make it. This was their *If Tube Lines Were People* personification sketch which proved to be their breakthrough, leading to them making online sketches for BBC3, which they produce themselves with Andrew Nolan filming and editing. Meg explains, 'Generally, we'd send off a bunch of ideas. Then they'll say yes or no to a few. We'd write it, get all the props and costumes, be in it, edit it afterwards. Then BBC3 would upload it, so essentially our work then had a better platform.'

Animals are even more commonly personified than things. For example, in a radio sketch, Mitchell & Webb have two pit ponies talking about their weekend. Robert Webb's cheery pony asks David Mitchell's dour pony if he 'saw the match' and Mitchell's pony expresses surprise that he even knows what a 'match' is, given that they spend most of their lives underground. In stand-up, Kat Williams voices the thoughts of the tiger who, in a real-life news story, mauled a man who climbed into their enclosure in a zoo, and Jerry Seinfeld imagines what horses must be thinking when raced around a circular track. Following the 'big hurry' they find out to their bemusement that they're back where they started from. Michelle Wolf too has a thread of personification running through her *Joke Show* special including at one point imagining a seal consenting to sex with an otter on the basis that the hybrid offspring would be the cutest animal ever. Bridget Christie even performed a whole stand-up set as an ant.

Like radio and stand-up, improvisation is an area where talking animals and things can be very simply conjured up in collaboration with the audience's imagination. I asked improviser Katy Schutte how much personification she does and she told me:

This week I have mainly been a dragon and a velociraptor in the shows that I've done. So, lots! The Maydays do a show called *Happily Never After* that's a homage [to] the likes of Tim Burton and Lemony Snicket. A show might not even have a human in it. It could just be a bunch of objects. Or we've had ones where paintings and objects come to life. I heard a nice idea that if you're going to play a lamp, play an angry lamp. Have an emotional state or a point of view. There's a nice exercise from [writer, producer and improviser] Richard Talerico, who's amazing, where everyone are objects that are in the same room, like in an old house, and then you chat between yourselves. You already have an idea of what the clock is going to be like: a bit old and grouchy or nostalgic or worrying about the future. The fireplace is probably going to be cosy and family orientated.

Personification is also a mainstay of animation. Steve Kaplan coaches animators and he told me that one of the scenes he'll show them is from *Chicken Little* where in a crucial baseball game, the coach desperately sends hopeless Little up to bat. As Steve observes:

> You can have a crazy person doing crazy absurd things as long as someone has got a grasp of reality in the scenario. So, you can't have Mork without Mindy. The coach is crazy here, so where is the sane character reacting to that? There isn't one. There has to be somebody else in the scenario because I cannot care about the crazy person. My problem with the animators here is it's all top-down writing. They're pushing the characters around. Rather than have Chicken Little be a striver who fears that he can't succeed, and yet, despite all odds he does, they have him be an idiot who for no good reason hits the ball and then slides, and he should be out, but he's not. It's designed incorrectly. That's why people don't care. The cumulative effect is it's an unsuccessful film. But if you take a look at any Pixar film, they come from character, everything they personify has a person's point of view. In animation, even if it's an anthropomorphic chicken, your character has to be a human being.

So, you can *change why*, *change when*, *change where*, *change who*, *change what*, *change how*, *reverse it*, *rescale it or personify it*, but don't lose sight of the human truth at the heart of the situation. Finally, I didn't revisit *change how* from our opening exercise and so for completeness, I offer the wonderfully absurd online sketch *How Animals Eat*. In a kind of reverse personification, they project animal qualities onto a human. The commitment required here is the precise opposite of that which Steve Kaplan discusses. Rather than committing to making an animal or thing recognizably human, they're committing to making a human recognizably animal! In the sketch, two men sit at a dinner table with one demonstrating to the other 'how animals eat' in increasingly ludicrous and cartoonish ways. The man witnessing all this is entirely deadpan, eating normally, again illustrating the importance of the reacting character and also indeed how little they need to do. A raised eyebrow can be enough. Here, his controlled non-reactions make the scene hilarious in a way it wouldn't be without a second person in the scene.

So in this middle section of the book, we've covered the games you play in your comedy and the worlds you can play in; sketch, scene and routine structure; the behaviour and interaction of characters; and finally more outlandish 'what if' scenarios. In the closing section we turn our attention to characters and scenes in full-length narratives from TV sitcom and comedy drama to stand-up shows and long-form improv.

PART THREE

Show

Chapter 8
Bosses, Strivers and Fools

At Bath Spa University in a combined group of BA Comedy and third-year acting students, we create, devise, write and film six 22-minute sitcoms. I lead the creating and writing process alongside Pat Welsh before handing over to the Film and Television department to take care of the shooting. The shows are filmed in multi-camera format in front of a live studio audience in the university's ridiculously high-spec TV studio. It's a wonderfully stimulating and intense project. When we spoke for this book, Pat explained:

> Those engaged in the sitcom project are third-year students and they have developed an acting methodology, strong skills in comic characterization drawing on the archetypes of *commedia dell'arte*, comedic performance skills geared towards performing in front of a live audience and a practical understanding of comedy structure. The sitcom project presents some key challenges – firstly how to achieve an extended narrative through the development of plot lines, secondly how to develop modern characters that translate to screen and thirdly how to navigate the twin objectives of playing to a live audience and to the camera.

What makes it possible to create six groups of characters in a matter of weeks that work together and function in a sitcom, is my *boss–striver–fool* model. These three character types, when put together, create a balanced, funny ensemble. The main character, the comic protagonist, will be a *striver*. As their name suggests, they are wanting to better themselves and improve their lives. They are not skilful or effective in achieving this end (if they were, there'd be no comedy). The boss is the one with authority, from whatever source (job role, position, social status, family role). Usually the authority figures in sitcoms are incompetent or dysfunctional in some way or exercise their authority badly. The fools are self-explanatory, but they needn't necessarily be stupid (although they often are.) They could be intelligent but still be a *fool* due to being naive, awkward or socially inept. In *Friends*, Monica is often (neurotically) in charge and so she is a boss. Ross and Rachel are our central strivers and Chandler's witty reactions to the others make him a foil, while Joey and Phoebe are our main fools. It is a common strategy to have a *foil* who is the voice-of-reason. They are the one the audience can relate to. For example, in *The Young Ones*, with its three grotesque central characters, early on they had to introduce Mike as a voice-of-reason to have someone more grounded who could stop the whole situation imploding.

Pat said that in the university context:

The boss–striver–fool model helps because it takes away some of the anxiety faced by inexperienced sitcom writers. It offers a clear template in which to create characters and develop relationships. Exemplars can be explored from extant sitcoms, giving the students confidence in this approach. This year we produced six sitcoms all based around start-up app businesses – which included dating, takeaway food delivery and dockless bike hire apps – and despite following the same model the students achieved very different characterizations, drawing on their individual observations and creative interpretation of the boss–striver–fool roles. The secret is to give individual characters clearly defined overt objectives and place obstacles in their paths that they are forced to negotiate.

The rest of this chapter has a sitcom/comedy drama focus, but you will also find bosses, strivers and fools quite naturally arising in all forms of comedy. For example, in the *Monty Python* Spam sketch we discussed in Chapter 4, the waitress is the *boss*, she is running things and will not compromise on the establishment's 'spam with everything' ethos. (She is not a sane, reasonable or effective boss of course; she simply wields the power in the situation.) The *striver* is the woman trying to get a dish without spam, and while she is the voice-of-reason, she not skilful or diplomatic in voicing her objection. The *fools* are her husband and indeed the Vikings, who are cheerfully going along with the madness (as fools often do). The *striver* is stuck between bosses and fools, which is the classic place to find this kind of character. And in the Spanish Inquisition sketch, Michael Palin's Cardinal Ximénez is the *boss* in the scenario, Terry Jones as Biggles is the *striver*, desperate to get it right, and the gurning Terry Gilliam as the third cardinal is the *fool*. In a stand-up context, in Chapter 5 I discuss Richard Pryor's extraordinary heart attack routine in which the *boss* is the heart attack, the *fool* is the operator of the heavenly call centre and, stuck in the middle, *striving* to stay alive, is Pryor himself.

On Steve Kaplan's recommendation I've been watching the splendid *Kominsky Method* on Netflix. Created by Chuck Lorre, it follows the titular venerable Hollywood acting coach, played by Michael Douglas, as he faces the realities of ageing, affectionately squabbles with his long-time agent and friend, struggles with his daughter and dates one of his more mature students. As I was watching, it struck me as a good example of my boss–striver–fool, plus foil, model.

BOSS: Alan Arkin as Norman Newlander, Sandy's agent and friend.

STRIVER: Michael Douglas as Sandy Kominsky, a once successful actor who now works as a revered acting coach in Hollywood.

FOIL: Sarah Baker as Mindy, Sandy's daughter, who runs his acting studio with him, and Nancy Travis as Lisa, a recent divorcée who decides to take acting lessons from Sandy and is Sandy's love interest.

FOOL: Lisa Edelstein as Phoebe, Norman's estranged and outrageous daughter who struggles with addictions. Other fools are to be found amongst the acting students.

It's a realist, naturalistic show, shot like a drama, with warmth and heart, and it also has some genuine things to teach. Steve Kaplan told me:

In the last episode, for a variety of reasons, they're kicking Michael Douglas out of his own studio and his daughter has booked the real Allison Janney to teach an acting class. It was funny but I agreed with her point of view. She says if you read a script and you identify with the protagonist, if you empathize with it, then it's *you*. If you read a script and you don't identify with the character or empathize with them, then it's somebody that you know. The more specific you can make the character, the better it will be compared to some generic person. A great example of that is *All in the Family*. Norman Lear took the British sitcom *Till Death Us Do Part* and he adapted it for American television. You already have the building blocks, a clash of opinions, clash of values, age and class, but the character of Archie Bunker is *his* father. His mother was Edith Bunker. Then there's that great collaboration with the perfect actor and that's luck partly, but what makes that show so good is the fact that it wasn't just, 'Okay, this right-wing bigot is arguing with his left-wing son-in-law'; it's about somebody that you know, somebody who is actually a vibrant vital part of you that you can't get rid of even if you wanted to.

This boss–striver–fool and foil dynamic recurs across so many sitcoms. I'm not saying the authors were thinking of it in exactly this way, but sitcom characters do tend to fall into this pattern. For example, the central trio of *Frasier* breaks down neatly into Martin Crane as a boss, Frasier as a striver and Niles as a fool (the intelligent but socially awkward kind). Daphne joins the central trio and, as a down-to-earth character who is exasperated by Frasier's pretension and snobbery, she is a foil (as well as being a funny character in her own right). From

Frasier, let's turn to another farcical show and one of the all-time greats: *Fawlty Towers*. Who is the boss in *Fawlty Towers*? It's Sybil, right? She is the one who is in charge, who Basil fears, and it's thanks to her that the hotel actually stays open. Basil is the striver whose struggles the show revolves around. He's striving for social status, a better class of guest and a quiet life. The central fool is Manuel, the hapless Spanish waiter, and there are other fools around like the Major, Miss Tibbs and Miss Gatsby. There are other bosses too who come into individual episodes, like Mrs Richards with her vase in 'Communication Problems', Mrs Chase with her Shih Tzu dog in 'The Kipper and The Corpse' and the American Mr Hamilton wanting his 'Waldorf Salad'. The regular foil is Polly; she is the voice-of-reason. Polly is a young woman, starting relationships and working on her ambition to be an artist. She is the one the audience can readily identify with and whose dilemma we can relate to. She is stuck in the middle and often having to cover up for Basil or getting embroiled in his schemes and deceptions. Crucially she is a low-status character. If she were high-status, she could put a stop to the nonsense. As it is, she is a hapless pawn. So, in *Fawlty Towers* we find:

BOSS – Sybil

STRIVER – Basil

FOIL – Polly

FOOL – Manuel

Despite repeated attempts, American remakes of *Fawlty Towers* fell far short of the original. A more recent UK classic, however, has had a highly successful remake in the States. Here's how the characters break down across the UK/US versions of *The Office*:

BOSS – Chris Finch/Todd Packer and Neil Godwin/Josh Porter

STRIVER – David Brent/Michael Scott

FOIL – Tim/Jim and Dawn/Pam

FOOL – Gareth/Dwight

The point of this model is to give you a leg-up when you're creating your own show. As you develop your own sitcom characters, ask yourself: who is the big comic character at the heart of the show? The absurd or badly behaved or eccentric focus of it all? This is your main striver, the protagonist. In the UK/US *The Office*, David Brent/Michael Scott is the 'striver' (he may be a manager in the hierarchy but he is not a 'boss' in status, and he is also the central protagonist whose striving is at the heart of the comedy). Who is the more normal character the audience relate to? It's Tim/Jim – the relatable everyman, the voice-of-reason, who feels the pain of Brent/Scott's antics. His beloved Dawn/Pam is also a foil, who provides a romantic plot strand which gives the show a bit of heart and developed way beyond the British original in the American version. Who fancies who in your show?

Then who has power over your central character? This is the boss. It might literally be a boss like Godwin/Porter (and later Ryan Howard and Charles Miner in the US *Office*). Godwin/Porter is a classic example of a character who is too good to be true and winds up the flawed central striver. Your boss needn't literally be a workplace 'boss': it can be anyone with power (social, familial, etc.), like the social power of Chris Finch/Todd Packer. Then ask yourself, who is the fool your protagonist has to deal with? Here, Gareth/Dwight is the central fool. There are other fools around too, like Keith/Kevin, whose character grew in the second series of the UK *Office* when viewers enjoyed the originally minor character's hopeless, lumpen presence.

Whilst it's most common for the central character to be a striver, in Donald Glover's *Atlanta*, Glover's character Earn is often the foil, reacting to the absurdities around him. Jerry occupies a similar position in *Seinfeld*. *Blackadder* is another interesting case to consider, with its shifting cast of characters from series to series. In the first *Blackadder*, written by Rowan Atkinson and Richard Curtis, Blackadder himself was the fool, which is very unusual for a central character. A fool rarely has enough depth to anchor the whole situation. This expensive production was considered a flop at the time and the BBC only agreed to a second series on a much reduced budget, meaning the lavish settings and outdoor action with horses were reduced to studio audience sitcom scale with a new writing team of Ben Elton and Richard Curtis (who'd co-scripted Atkinson's breakthrough live sketch show).

Tellingly, in the second series, Blackadder was shifted (in my terms) from fool to striver. Completing the central cast were the boss Queen Elizabeth I and the fool Baldrick (and Percy). In the court we find our foil Melchett and another fool, Nursey. In the third *Blackadder*, the boss became the Prince Regent. Blackadder is of course again the striver, with Baldrick the fool and various foils

When we come to *Blackadder Goes Forth*, the foil Captain Darling is also a rival of Blackadder. Yes, your foil might be a rival rather than a more reluctantly co-operative character like Polly in *Fawlty Towers*. And there are two bosses in the fourth series: General Melchett and Field Marshall Haig. The fools double up too with Baldrick and George. Although both are fools, one is working class and the other upper class.

So, with the boss–striver–fool model you can double up some or all of the slots as we do with the Bath Spa sitcoms. But note that you'd be hard pressed to find a successful show where two characters were basically the same. If this is the case in your embryonic script, make them different – or merge them! I could go on giving examples of bosses, strivers, foils and fools in sitcom, and indeed when I teach this model in class, students spontaneously start shouting out sitcoms and everyone figures out who is a boss, a striver, a fool or a foil. So many sitcoms have this dynamic at their heart.

Building an ensemble of characters

To illustrate the kind of process you might work through with your own show, let's build a cast for an imaginary sitcom inspired by (okay, ripped off from) *The Kominsky Method*. I'm calling it 'The La Tête Method' and I'm going to make the central character comedy coach Christian La Tête. (See what I did there?) He's our striver/protagonist and, clearly, I'm basing him on, ahem, myself. Exaggerating the truth just a little bit, let's say he takes comedy very seriously and seldom laughs; a chin-scratching analytical response being his reaction to anything comedic. Now let's use the positives and negatives my partner Kate attributed to *me* in Chapter 1 and say that Christian is affectionate, decisive and impractical. Let's make Kate herself the foil, but she'll be the version of Kate I knew when we first met. I was actually her comedy teacher! I think I'll call the character Cathy Chedworth (partly because Kate can't stand being called Cathy), and in the longer arc of the show Christian and Cathy can get together as Kate and I did. With a sitcom ensemble, you're always looking to tie your characters together so they can naturally keep interacting, so, in this case, we want to tie her more into the world of the show. As well as being a student, she can also be doing admin work for La Tête. In return for this, she can get free places on the courses, which can lead to some entertaining friction. Let's make her a bit younger than La Tête and say she makes weird online short-form comedy bits for TikTok (or whatever app is the latest thing) that Christian doesn't get.

Who could have power over La Tête and be the boss of the piece? Let's say it's his business partner Violet Delaney, the brains behind his comedy studio operation. Some years prior to making comedy my full-time work, I had a part-time admin job in a college and I'm going to base the boss of our sitcom on my boss – an exaggerated fictionalized version of her, I hasten to add in case she's reading. Violet will have a very positive friendly side, but this could change in an instant to her reign-of-terror side. So, there is a constant fear of the other side even when she's being nice. Plus, her love of business jargon and attitudes are (and were) incongruous in an arts setting and will certainly wind up La Tête.

Now we need a fool. One of my very first jobs was working in a supermarket in the fruit and veg department. There was an eager-to-please but rather hopeless older man that I worked alongside. (When he first encountered mangetout, he memorably pronounced it 'mango trout'.) Being hopeless and eager to please is a good combination, as he can cause more problems than if he were just lazy and disengaged (and you want active characters, not passive ones). Let's give him the role of La Tête's intern who is shadowing him and learning about the world of comedy. He can be named Magnus Trout. Let's make him sixty, so an incongruous age to be an intern. He's taken early retirement and is a devotee of an older generation of comedians that La Tête is disdainful of. He also attempts to do comedy which La Tête considers hopelessly outmoded. This traps La Tête between a younger character (Cathy) and an older character (Magnus), neither of whose comedy enthusiasms he understands, which feels like a good place to put him. So here is our line-up of characters:

BOSS: Business manager Violet Delaney

STRIVER: Comedy coach Christian La Tête

FOIL: Student, admin and app comedy video maker Cathy Chedworth

FOOL: Intern and old-school style aspiring comic Magnus Trout

Let's now turn to a real-world example of developing characters and a situation for a TV comedy narrative. Following online and film festival success, Steve Whiteley has now developed his comedy short *Swiped* into a sitcom script with Channel 4 and Hat Trick Productions, working with executive producer Matt Tiller and myself. As Steve explains, 'The pitch document we developed consisted of a six-episode synopsis, a character breakdown and what the overall arc of the series would be. Matt sent out to broadcasters and Channel 4 eventually commissioned a pilot script.' I am script-editing what became 'Woke Heroes' (a punning take on 'folk heroes') and at the time of writing we're waiting to hear if we'll get the green light to film a pilot. When we spoke, Steve said that the *Swiped* project was 'a prime example of the need to act on things. If you've got an idea, just go and do it. I have lots of ideas swirling around but it's usually the ones that won't leave you alone that are the ones to act on. The idea that keeps coming back to you.'

From the start we worked with the intention that the short film would also function as a taster for a sitcom. You'll recall that the premise was that moped riding youths in London were swiping phones from people in order to make them more present. Logically it seemed to work better if our characters were the originators of the moped phone theft racket and they had the honourable intention of improving people's lives, but subsequent copycats had stolen their idea and corrupted it. Steve recalled, 'Then it was about fleshing out the characters and fleshing out their world, asking where do they come from, who are their families?' My boss–striver–fool model helped here. The characters are the swipers Jordan and Talia (strivers), Ryan (fool) and Jordan's parents Janet and Neil (bosses), and they all live together on a deprived inner London council estate. Steve adds, 'We made Neil Jordan's stepdad, which allows for some nice friction between the two of them.' When you're developing character relationships, always look to increase the friction.

As he develops characters, Steve draws on observations of others as well as on his own life and experiences:

> I'll try and create characters from people I know. I'll think, maybe I can take a bit of that friend, and there's an attribute that another friend of mine has got that'd be quite funny if we add it to this character. A character might be taken from three or four different people. I'll try and create characters as much as possible from people I already know, or know of, rather than start completely from scratch, otherwise they can easily come across as unbelievable. Then with Jordan being into meditation, that would've come from me, as I'm big into meditation. I wanted to bring some Buddhist philosophy into this world because it's a juxtaposition that you would never usually see. I was really motivated by the idea of portraying these young kids, in a comedic way, in a positive light.

Actors help flesh out characters too. For example, in the original *The Office*, Ricky Gervais and Stephen Merchant initially envisaged the character of Gareth as a big, tough, shaven-headed 'squaddie' type, and in a genius left-field casting move skinny, boggle-eyed McKenzie Crook landed the role. With the character of Ryan in *Swiped* (like Gareth, a 'fool'), he really became a fleshed out individual when Steve cast actor Selom Awadzi in the short, who brought his distinctive physical comedy to the role. Steve remarks, 'A lot of stuff also happened on the shoot too. Over those three days, we improvised bits and that also helped develop the characters.' Reflecting on going from short-form to long-form comedy narratives, Steve told me:

> I started making the YouTube sketches, then moved into performing regularly on the stand-up circuit as myself and as [pompous urban poet] Wisebowm. If I think back to the Wisebowm Edinburgh shows when first I came to you Chris, they were just a collection of comedy rhymes. Then you wisely pushed it in the direction of turning the show into a narrative. The Edinburgh Fringe was probably my first experience of developing a long-form narrative, which then led to the Radio 4 show. Writing for radio was very different to anything else I'd done and it was a great learning curve as the writing needs to be so descriptive because it's not a visual medium. That experience definitely helped me write the Channel 4 sitcom pilot 'Woke Heroes', which came from *Swiped*. I understand structure better now and I have these character Bibles for each character. What's their point of view? How do people see them? How do they

perceive other people? What's their traits, backgrounds? When I first started off, it was very much like, 'Oh, here's an idea. I'm just going to start writing dialogue.' There was no structure to it whatsoever; it's taken me a long time to learn that. Throughout the Edinburgh shows, there was lots of improv too. I had that skill set for that because I'd done improv on and off for years. And I still incorporate improv wherever possible into what I'm doing. Now where I'm trying to go with it, as you and I have discussed, is using my improv skills but in a solitary way. How can I use that muscle on my own? I tend to go for walks now and when things come up, I'll start recording them into my phone. I've also started to experiment doing dialogue between characters and recording that. All those skills are things I've learned through doing these various things over the last six, seven years, though at the time you don't know where it's all going. You're just doing it. You're driven by passion. It's really important as well to keep learning. I'm constantly reading. But really, the best thing you can [do is] go out and live your life, because that's where most of the stuff comes from. For me, I seem to get myself in the most random situations and that ends up being material.

Other models of character relationships

Lucy Lumsden commissioned stand-up Lee Mack's sitcom *Not Going Out* for the BBC. The central character is based on Mack's stand-up persona and from there he built a group of characters around him. Lucy told me, 'Lee, knew that he needed a confidante so you have Tim Vine being his mate. Then you have his polar opposite which is Sally Bretton's character, who is always going to see through him, and we are going to enjoy that. Then a fool in Katie Wix character. I think it's gloriously simple in a way as long as your central figure is someone the audience wants to spend time with.' Lucy says that you can look at the characters you're populating your own world with as highlighting different aspects of the central character in this way: 'Which characters are going to help me show which sides of their personality? Who's going to challenge them and show us all their defence mechanisms? Seeing those defence mechanisms is where so much of the comedy lies. You'll add in a parent or someone they've got to impress, and then somebody who's even more stupid than they are.' In effect, bosses and fools. 'I think you see that a lot. Who's going to be my confidante? Who's going to test me? Then, I need someone I either fancy, or I hate. You definitely have that in *Not Going Out*.'

There are lots of models of comedy characters out there. Assuming you're not already writing about a family, another model is to treat all the characters *as if* they were a family. Let's say your show is set in an office. The dysfunctional *bosses* in your organization are the parents, your *strivers* are like the older kids, with the *fools* as younger kids. You might even have grandparents, old hands in the job who bring some eccentricity, and aunts and uncles too. And Pat Welsh says, 'Scott Sedita's "Eight Characters of Sitcom" also provides a useful reference point as exemplars can be identified in contemporary sitcoms.' When we work together with the Bath Spa students, my boss–striver–fool model happily works with other character models, like Sedita's. To show how, here are Scott Sedita's 'Eight Characters of Sitcom' and ways I see my bosses, strivers, fools – and a foil – slotting into his model:

> The Logical Smart One – could be a striver or a foil (but probably not a boss, unless you want a good boss!)
> The Lovable Loser – would be a great striver
> The Neurotic – a boss or a striver, or if taken to an extreme, a fool
> The Dumb One – it's the fool!
> The Bitch/Bastard – a boss or a striver
> The Womanizer/Manizer – a striver, or could be a fool if they are truly hopeless
> The Materialistic One – striver or boss
> In Their Own Universe – the fool again, or would be a pleasingly disastrous boss

Steve Kaplan's *The Comic Hero's Journey* offers his own model of comedy movie character archetypes: the fool, the voice-of-reason, the innocent, the animal, the trickster and the magical object of desire. Two of these we already have: the *fool* and the *voice-of-reason* (the foil). Here are the others and where I see them potentially slotting into my model:

> The innocent – can be a good foil, but also could be a striver or a fool or even a naive boss – so across-the-board useful.
> The animal – could be a striver or a fool – or a very worrying boss.
> The trickster – a great striver character; think Blackadder.
> The magical object of desire (particularly found in romcoms) is a boss due to the power they have over the striver.

A recent classic show with a 'magical object of desire' was series 2 of *Fleabag*, where we find the 'Hot' Priest. Fleabag herself is the striver and, completing the main cast, the Godmother played by Olivia Colman is a boss and Fleabag's sister Claire and her husband are fools. But of course, 'the magical object of desire' might not even be a person. It could be any glittering and borderline unattainable prize that drives your striver's actions. In *Only Fools and Horses* it's the talismanic sum of a million pounds: as Del Boy (the striver) would say to his brother Rodney (the foil), 'This time next year we'll be millionaires.' Among the bosses was more wealthy business rival Boycie and crucially their dead mother who, through Del Boy, exerted her authority from beyond the grave. The central fool was originally Granddad and later Uncle Albert, and in the wider cast Trigger. When we do the university sitcom project at Bath Spa, one of the questions I keep asking early on as the characters are developing is 'Who do you know who is like this?' If they say, 'No one' (and often they do), then they have to work harder to find models for the character. It's often the *fools* for whom they can't find a real-life analogue. That's because it's so easy to make someone stupid (if you're going down the stupid fool route) that they often end up so off-the-scale stupid and so incredibly inept, that you think no real person could be like this and still function. As soon as the fools draw on real-life stupidity, not only do they become more believable, they also become funnier. As you get into character models and archetypes, it's important to keep bringing it back to real people. In *Only Fools*, David Jason based his portrayal of Del Boy on a real-life East End of London wheeler-dealer he'd known, Derek Hockley.[1] This is another example of an actor bringing something to the role – like Mackenzie Crook as Gareth in *The Office* – that the writers hadn't anticipated. In this case, writer John Sullivan imagined Del Boy being scruffy and overweight but, drawing on the real Derek, David Jason saw Del Boy as a dapper cockney with gold rings and bracelets.

Commedia dell'arte is another useful model of an ensemble of characters. *Commedia* developed in Italy in the early sixteenth century and spread throughout Europe, influencing Shakespeare, Molière, opera, vaudeville, musical theatre and now modern comedy. Steve Kaplan discusses *commedia* in his books and when we spoke he told me:

> As I'm working on comedy and as I'm writing the books, it just becomes clearer and clearer to me that Western comedy all comes out of this movement to have a character being in the lead as opposed to plot. Aristotle says that *plot* is the most important thing. But with the fall of Rome in the Dark Ages, there were no playwrights, there were no directors, there were no theatres. With *commedia*, they were just roaming bands of actors, and what did they have? All they had were stories from the Bible, or scenarios and characters. The characters created everything. Now, maybe this is a reaction to all the method acting training I took as a young man (that luckily or unluckily didn't take hold with me), but one of the things that was clear to me, was the fact that they were so afraid of us playing stereotypes. And yet if you look at comedy, especially sketch comedy, how long do we have to communicate to the audience who the character is? We have seconds. And what makes a successful sitcom? A character comes in and you immediately know, '*This* is

---

[1] 'David Jason: "His Only Fools and Horses secrets"', *Daily Mirror*, 8 September 2011, https://www.mirror.co.uk/tv/tv-news/david-jason-his-only-fools-and-horses-152413.

going to happen.' Kramer coming through the door, and you know where this is going. If you put a Chandler and Joey in a room with beautiful women, Chandler is going to be nervous but be very verbal and Joey is going to be stupid and overoptimistic. It writes itself because the characters are so clear. With *Everybody Loves Raymond*, if Deborah wants to take the family Christmas photo without Marie, and if you know the characters, you know that there's going to be a war. The *commedia* has all these typical characters and all you had to do was put them on stage together and something would happen. If you look at comedy today, like *commedia*, we still have the fool, we have the innocent, we have the trickster, we have the wise guy, we have the mentor. And if you think of successful sitcoms, you can ascribe those parts to the characters.

Pat Welsh teaches *commedia* to our comedy students at Bath Spa University and as he does so, like Kaplan, he relates the traditional characters to contemporary references: 'We develop a microcosm based around "two houses both alike in dignity".' That is, as per Romeo and Juliet, two families both of the same social standing. Pat continues, 'The patriarchs of the two families are the old men; the bosses: Pantalone the miserly and lecherous head of the household – a self-made man; a Mr Burns – and his counterpart the loquacious and glutinous doctor Il Dottore, who has all the airs and graces and the advantage of education but lacks the entrepreneurial spirit.' Pat's description of these two characters suddenly puts me in mind of Frasier and his father, who I suddenly saw as Il Dottore and Pantalone. I checked out this hunch, and, one bit of googling later, lo and behold, among the images on the fridge of the Frasier household who do we find? None other than Pantalone! A playful nod to the archetypes behind Frasier and his father? Pat adds, 'Both families have feckless and narcissistic offspring – the lovers – the types who populate the reality TV show *Made in Chelsea*. They are strivers in search of "love", although this is an entirely unrealistic romantic conceit. Plot lines often focus around them combating the impediment to their love – usually their parents, who oppose their union often for financial reasons. Then there's the machinations of the household servants – for example, Columbina, the voice-of-reason [the foil], aka Daphne in *Frasier*, and her servant suitor Arlecchinno, who is driven by his belly and his wandering eye [the fool], aka Joey from *Friends*.'

Pat concluded, 'I also often reference John Vorhaus's concept of "comic perspective" – the lens through which a character views the world. He says, "Show me a character without a comic perspective and I'll show you a straight man." I impress upon the students the necessity to wear their hearts on their sleeves, so to speak, and ensure that the audience can identify with the character from the get go – from the moment they walk on stage or onto the set. This is a combination of physicality and vocality and a defining characteristic that the audience can relate to.'

There are many other models of characters, as Steve Kaplan notes: 'Somebody else says everybody in the cast is a member of Winnie the Pooh's Hundred Acre Wood. Who's your Tigger, who's your Eeyore? Or somebody says everybody is in the *Wizard of Oz*. Who's your Dorothy? Who's your Lion? Who's your Scarecrow? There's lots of ways of dividing it, but it all comes back to talking about our typical essential characterizations.'

Likeable and dislikeable characters

Finally, writers often get feedback that their characters aren't likeable enough. Yet at the same time there are many sitcoms with characters who behave badly and aren't obviously likeable. Indeed, we can have an appalled fascination for truly dark characters like Jill from Julia Davis's sitcom *Nighty Night*. Davis describes Jill as the ultimate extreme narcissist and sociopath, and acknowledges they're traits she's interested in and that run through a lot of her characters. Davis's horrific creations are in fact based on real people! She says she does see such people around and continues to be shocked by their behaviour and wants to keep looking at it from a slightly different perspective each show she makes.[2] Even if you're not creating truly dark, sociopathic characters, you will probably have some badly behaved, even appalling, people in your show. How do you deal with dislikeable characters when likeability is so valued?

I asked Lucy Lumsden, who commissioned Davis to make period comedy *Hunderby* while she was head of comedy at Sky, how people can get away with having absolutely objectionable characters at the heart of a show. She replied, 'That becomes the comedy of, "Thank God it's not me!" There's a complete flip from, "I'm going to connect" to voyeurism, and you just want to see how far someone can push it. There's huge pleasure to be gained from that. Jill in *Nighty Night* is abhorrent, so you're not demanding that the whole of the audience fall in love with her. You are celebrating the fact that a lot of the audience won't. You're flipping it. And Basil Fawlty is horrific, isn't he? Edina from *Ab Fab* [*Absolutely Fabulous*] is another one. It's the joy of seeing someone being that outrageous.'

Dislikeable characters can also be engaging for the audience as wish fulfilment. By which I mean, the character does behave appallingly (by society's standards) but does the kinds of things we, the audience, would love to do if we were bold/ reckless enough: for example, Blackadder, Fleabag and Larry David in *Curb*.

---

[2] B. Dowell, 'Julia Davis reveals the anger that went into creating her fabulously ghastly comedy monster in Sally4Ever', *Radio Times*, 25 October 2018, https://www.radiotimes.com/news/tv/2018-10-25/julia-davis-reveals-the-anger-that-went-into-creating-her-fabulously-ghastly-comedy-monster-in-sally4ever/.

They don't care and we love it. These characters do have positive qualities of course. All are articulate, bold and imaginative. You couldn't, however, have a cast made up entirely of these extreme types. Imagine if Jill, Basil and Edina were all in one show! They'd cancel each other out. You need the reasonable and normal people around them for contrast, but also to create a way in for the audience. You need the foils and the likeable characters with whom we'll relate and sympathize. Then, as we'll discuss in the next chapter, once you've created your rich ensemble of characters, you don't need to strain to come up with funny ideas; just put your characters in a situation and watch them go.

Chapter 9

Characters Driving the Narrative

In a long-form improv show you probably won't want to spend time at the start with all the characters meeting each other for the first time. As an improviser, even when you have no idea who the other characters are or what your relationships are, a good approach is to act as if you do. You play the scene as if there is a whole set of established relationships which gradually become revealed to you, the player, as the scene unfolds. This is much more interesting for the audience than watching a lot of introductions. And the same applies to scripted comedy. But if a sitcom is set in a business of some kind, in my experience, newer writers will tend to make the first episode the grand opening. Similarly, if it's a flat share (one of the most pitched situations) then episode 1 is them all moving in together. Is this the most interesting starting-point? Almost certainly not, but it's certainly the easiest, which is why people reach for it. It's more challenging to jump into the thick of a situation and still introduce the world and the characters to the audience – and all without them feeling spoon-fed. But, done well, it's so much more involving to watch.

That said, some stories *do* benefit from beginning at the beginning, as *Catastrophe* brilliantly did, but with other sitcoms that start with the 'how they met' or 'how it all began' episode – like *Spaced* and *One Foot in the Grave* – the first episode is often the least interesting one. (As these two were in otherwise brilliant series.) It can be better to just hit the ground running from the get-go with everything in place like *Fawlty Towers*, which opens with Sybil berating Basil for not hanging a picture that she's been on at him to get up on the wall. With that interaction, along with Basil being rude to some guests who didn't get their alarm call and Manuel not understanding basic instructions regarding breakfast trays, you have the whole situation laid out for you in miniature. The beauty of joining a situation that's already in play, is it's all had time to go stale and dysfunctional, which has much more potential for comedy than fresh beginnings. You may want to work out the 'how it all began' backstory – I'd suggest just don't bother actually writing it as an episode. A middle ground, between showing how it all began and presenting a fully formed world, is to introduce *one* character into the world. The first episode of *Friends* does this with the arrival of Rachel into the established world of the other characters, and even then she is from Monica's past, so is not a totally unknown quantity. That also has a practical function in that it allows Rachel to be plausibly assimilated into their world quickly, in a way we wouldn't accept of a stranger. This pilot episode is a masterclass in economically and clearly setting up characters and a world. Indeed, the first *three minutes* establishes all the characters and their distinct attitudes and personalities. Chandler makes quips, Phoebe cleanses Ross's aura, Joey suggests to Ross that in order to get over his heartbreak he should visit a strip club, Ross clumsily opens an umbrella as he goes to meet Rachel (who he is clearly smitten by), Rachel herself is spirited and self-involved, while Monica is taking charge and controlling. Indeed Monica, as a 'boss' who is in control of these opening minutes, is in a position to give the audience useful exposition: under the guise of filling in the friends, she explains that Ross has broken up with Carol and she introduces Rachel to everyone as her high school best friend. The other kind of exposition we get in these opening minutes is how the characters behave and react to each other. This is what you're aiming for – for all of your characters to be immediately clear and distinct from the outset and where exposition is needed for it to emerge naturally from the action. But how do you set about finding your central characters?

Finding your protagonists

Friends is the product of a writing team where there are a huge number of stories, experiences and ideas to draw on. Add in the producer, the script editor and anyone else offering ideas and notes, and suddenly you have a proliferation of possibilities. Clelia Mountford's company Merman's sitcom *Motherland* was the distillation of many ideas arising in this way, as she explains: 'It was based on everyone's experience. I've got kids, and we all threw in experiences of our own and we created this document of stories. In the early days, we had a writers room of stand-ups, who were parents, and who also came up with ideas and stories. Helen Linehan, whose idea it originally was, has got amazing stories from being a mother. Graham Linehan worked on the first series, but the second series was all women writing. With the second series, Holly Walsh and Sharon Horgan wrote together, and Helen and Barunka O'Shaughnessy wrote together. They each wrote three scripts and then swapped over and made notes on each other's scripts.' The starting-point for this show generated a huge number of ideas to corral into these scripts. So how do you boil down this great mass of possible ideas into characters, scenes and stories?

When it comes to telling a story, the first question to answer is, whose story is it? Sometimes you know already who your central characters are and sometimes you need to find them. *Fawlty Towers* is a classic example of a sitcom based on observation of a real situation: the Gleneagles Hotel in Torquay where the Pythons were staying while doing location filming. The story goes that the hotel was so bad that everyone left, apart from John Cleese and Connie Booth who stayed to observe the situation. Basing Basil and Sybil on Mr and Mrs Sinclair who ran the hotel, John Cleese says all they changed were the sizes; in real life Mrs Sinclair was the more sizeable of the two. The central characters were there from the start. Whereas with a show like *Motherland*, well, when we begin we know our central character will be a mother (or mothers) – but *who* are they? Long-form improv, where the possibilities are similarly legion including input from the audience and all the ideas and life experience of the various players, offers a helpful perspective on finding your protagonists.

One of the first long-form shows I saw was Impromptu Shakespeare with my daughter Kaia and my partner Kate, where the company created a recognizably Shakespearean narrative based upon random audience suggestions that were written on ping-pong balls and thrown onto the stage. While it wasn't all in verse (that would be a tall order), it was strongly Shakespearean in characters, language, narrative and themes. It was also funny, dramatic and had a satisfying plot. We all thoroughly enjoyed it. I didn't doubt it was entirely improvised but I did assume that beforehand they would have agreed certain parameters, like ,'You're going to be the king, you're going to be the fool, we'll be the lovers', but when I asked one of the company, Rebecca MacMillan, about this afterwards she said, 'No, there was nothing agreed.' I thought, 'Wow, how do they do that?'

In some long-form improv formats you *do* agree characters in advance, like in the improvised *Sherlock* show that Rebecca plays in alongside the artistic director of the Bristol Improv Theatre, Caitlin Campbell. Here they agree who's playing Holmes and Watson beforehand (for costume reasons as much as anything else). Where a show has no roles agreed beforehand, Rebecca told me, 'There's a feedback process that's happening live with improv where the audience is a player in it as well. You can tell when they really like a character.' So, the audience have a hand in identifying the protagonist. Caitlin adds, 'It's always obvious to an audience, but if they're new to improvisation it's not necessarily obvious to the improvisers on stage. I think the trick to it is to have very clear, bold choices early on, so you work out who the protagonist is. Who is the person that we care about and that we want to follow? Once you've worked out who your protagonist is, it's a simple question of "What matters to that person and what do they want?"'

Working on a written script it's similarly a case of asking: who are we liking? Who's fun to talk about and write about? Or when you're thinking of real-life models for your characters, what are the most striking and memorable qualities of those people? In a written script, in your early drafts, you might be focusing on the wrong character. Be prepared to switch if your readers or collaborators are more engaged by another character, or you're simply finding another character more absorbing and fun to write. Or maybe this script doesn't go anywhere and rather than binning the whole thing, there might be a character who could become the protagonist in a fresh script.

Long-form improvisation

There'll be more insights from the world of long-form improv in these last two chapters, so before we go on, let's take a a closer look at the form. There are many formats, and new ones are being invented all the time, but a typical approach is to seek audience suggestions just once, at the start of the show, and then improvise a narrative for 30 minutes, an hour or even 90 minutes, with an interval. Some formats have a set sequence of games and scenes like Free Association's excellent *Jacuzzi* shows, a late-night favourite at the Edinburgh Fringe, which has special guests who deliver a monologue that inspires a series of scenes, and of course there is the pioneering Harold format: a mix of scenes and games that reference each other and increasingly converge, now existing in multiple variations including the blind Harold which is played in the dark!

Then there are long-form improv shows that spontaneously create a narrative without a predetermined structure, either with no preconceived parameters or working within the contours of a given genre. Genre shows are especially popular in the UK, perhaps because improv is a newer form here and non-specialist audiences don't necessarily have an understanding of improv beyond seeing *Whose Line is it Anyway?* on TV, so having a show based on a genre like a musical, fantasy or murder mystery creates a way in and makes theatres more comfortable about programming it. Caitlin Campbell told me, 'I love genre improv because you get to play in a world, and play characters, that the audience recognizes and you can choose to play or subvert them. The really good genre shows are good because they're like a love letter to the genre.' With a genre improv show – like a murder mystery or a Shakespearian improv – you need to understand what the audience expects or wants from the kind of story you're doing. Improv teacher, performer and author Katy Schutte told me about a warm-up exercise that improvisers might do before this kind of show: 'There's a lovely exercise called "genre cauldron" where you sit around a circle and shout out all the things that you associate with the genre. With murder mysteries you would be like, "There's a denouement. There's probably family intrigue. Maybe some jewellery has gone missing. The detective will be eccentric in some way. Maybe they're Belgian."'

Rebecca MacMillan has recently joined a company improvising Dickensian tales. I asked her how much research this entailed and she replied, 'I read Dickens and watched some Dickens adaptations, because people's idea of the genre comes as much from famous costume dramas.' But as an improviser you have to be selective as to what you draw on, as Rebecca explains: 'His books often follow lots of different characters over a long time and in many places. To try and pack all that into an hour-and-three-quarter performance would be completely overwhelming. I guess it's distilling the essence of a Dickensian story, which is not the same thing as being true to Dickensian narrative structure.' Rebecca said of these kinds of shows, 'You have a complicity [with the audience] around how you achieve a satisfactory story that feels like a story in that genre.' Since starting to improvise Dickens, Rebecca began to notice a cross-contamination with the improvised Shakespeare performances: 'We found that a Dickens quality was coming into our Shakespeare stories! We had a couple of Shakespeare shows that were about a working person done good. Now that's very Dickens, but it's not going to happen in Shakespeare. You're not going to get the fruit seller becoming the king. We had to weed that out.'

If you're writing a script and it is a genre piece (film noir, western, sci-fi, etc.), then you also need to understand what the audience expect of it. Beyond that, whatever your style of show, you need to know what it is, what it does and what the audience wants from it. For instance, if Ben Elton and Richard Curtis were to write the often speculated-about fifth series of *Blackadder*, then the audience would have expectations of what that would be like. Blackadder has to be in an underling or servile role and he has to be cleverer than his superiors and rebellious too. Also, there's got to be a cunning plan from Baldrick along with anachronistic modern references in a historical setting. We the audience know what we want from a particular narrative and it's up to the writers (like the improvisers) to deliver that, but in a way that's not predictable or repetitive. Shows that run out of steam have often exhausted all the ways of doing what the audience wants them to do, and are then casting around anywhere and everywhere to find stories and situations.

Conversely, it might take a while for a show to discover what it actually is, as was the case with *Blackadder*, which didn't find its successful form until series 2. Rebecca agrees: 'Yes, you get these TV shows where people say "The first series is rubbish, watch it from season 2." The show itself had to discover what it is, in order for people to feel, "Now I know what the show is and why I like it."' This is one of the main challenges with writing your scripted comedy: figuring out exactly what it is and what the audience want it to do. You won't know yourself at the outset, but as you write you need to be alive to the things you (and the audience) are enjoying about it so that you can keep on doing it.

As well as genre shows, Caitlin Campbell – in common with the other improvisers I spoke to – also performs in free-form narrative shows that have no defined genre or tone. As she observes, 'It's the hardest thing to do because you have to work out the style that you're playing in while you're creating it. If you miss the mark on that, you never quite work out what kind of story you're telling. It needs very strong choices early on.' Improv troupe the RH Experience's show *Stuck!* is an example of one that isn't pegged to any genre. *Stuck!* tells a story of three characters trapped in circumstances inspired by audience suggestions. Their stories are fast-paced and absurd, ranging in tone from tragic to joyful, and the stories unfold using quick flashbacks and cutaways. I saw *Stuck!* at Soho Theatre and as well as admiring the skill and energy of the players and the spontaneous work of the accompanying musician, I was also conscious of the extent to which the lighting and sound technician was a creative player in the show, adding atmosphere, choosing when flashbacks happened and even wrong-footing the performers. Conor Jatter of the RH Experience told me:

> We've been working with our tech, Tom Bacon, for nearly twelve years now. So, he knows us like no one else and is so important to us, and to the shows. He's less our tech and more our director as he's got such a valuable outside eye, and is able to steer the show in the right direction from the tech booth. I personally think it's also vital, especially when performing an art form such as improv, to have someone that will keep you on your toes. If I'm ever feeling too comfortable, or that I feel like I know where a scene or show is going, then something's gone wrong. Tom tests our abilities, and yes, he can wrong-foot us, but it's always in a playful way, never malicious. He's pulling us and pushing us to see where we can take him next. I think one of the last things we say to him before we go on stage is 'Make us sweat Tom!' And I think that shows in our performance, as we play hard and fast, and we're very happy to throw something away quickly if it's not working, or go down a very different rabbit hole if something new begins to work.

I asked Caitlin if any of her shows have a similarly creative role for the tech and she told me:

> In *Murder She Didn't Write* our tech person, Alex Coyle, has been working with us for six years now, almost as long as we've been doing the show. He is such a voice in the show, and it's something that a lot of people comment on after they've seen it. There's a guideline in improv: 'show don't tell'. It's more exciting to see things happen than hear people talk about it. That's very difficult with a murder mystery, where the action is happening over a single day but referencing the events of many, many years of history between people. So we put in flashbacks, so you can see the victim talking to the suspects, and you can see what their motives were, rather than just hearing

them talked about. Alex is the one who gets to cue those flashbacks, so if he hears us say something like, 'I heard you arguing earlier today', or 'Well, I should be honest, our history wasn't exactly 100 per cent brilliant', then he can cue a flashback. He can also do it whenever he wants! You might have just said something you thought was fairly innocuous like, 'We were best friends', and suddenly you're in a flashback.

This finds an echo in scripted comedy where flashbacks or cutaways are used, often contradicting the main action. A character might say they had 'a quiet night' and we immediately see a quick cutaway of them in the thick of an outrageously hedonistic party. I asked Caitlin if their tech Alex would try and wrong-foot them as I'd seen the RH Experience tech do and she responded, 'Yes, absolutely. Alex is brutal with the really short edits. Sometimes, the lights will come up on a scene, and you'll only have the chance to say something like, "Listen, I brought you out here to the garden for a reason . . ." and then it's a blackout. We'll never know what that reason was, or we will find out in the next scene. It keeps you on your toes, which is really fun.'

Keep it simple

In the same way that scenes in a sitcom can be like sketches that also serve to advance the narrative, within long-form improvised shows the scenes can have many of the qualities of short-form scenes. Caitlin explains:

> Good scenes in a long-form narrative still have games in them. There's still a lot of play. Game in improv is sometimes talked about like it's quite complicated, but actually it's simply finding a shiny thing, and then playing with it until it's not fun any more. At BIT [the Bristol Improv Theatre] we teach escalation, we teach play and discovery, finding things that are fun in scenes and playing with them, and we do have a focus on narrative. For example, if a scene happens and no one has been changed by it, then why have we watched it? So, we have a rule called 'change or be changed'.

The same thinking applies in sitcom writing where every scene needs to have a purpose.

> If two characters are diametrically opposed, then you need to work out how a change can happen for the story to move on. We talk a lot in our beginner's improv classes about arguing on stage. Once you start arguing on stage, often you want to win the argument, and it's really easy to confuse winning the argument with winning the scene. In order for this to be a scene with a shared

reality, one of you needs to lose. If you are good at this, you'll learn how to enjoy these things, losing beautifully, losing dramatically, losing sexily. That's because you are on the same team performing for the audience. You are not on opposite teams, and you cannot win an improv scene . . . When training improvisers at BIT, we try and use the language of what makes it easier and what makes it harder. You learn that there are some choices that will make a scene harder because it will suddenly get confusing and you'll get lost or you won't be able to agree on what the reality of the world is. Then there are some choices that make it easier: you're on the same page, you know what matters, you know what's important. The hard scenes can still work and can still be funny, but we try and make things easy for ourselves. The things that allow that to happen are listening, supporting and accepting. Then the fourth one, my bonus on the list, is attempting to enjoy yourself. It's very hard to listen, support, or accept if you're not having a good time. Sometimes, you see beginner improvisers straining every muscle in their body, trying so hard to listen, and that tension actually stops you from listening. Being able to listen, support and accept comes from being able to relax on stage, which is a really tall order. I think it is why people take years before they're able to improvise something that looks really simple. Our instinct is to complicate things and bring in loads of stuff. When we panic, we reach outside of the story and bring in loads of other elements because we want the story to be exciting or interesting enough. The longer you do it, the more you learn that the simpler it is the better.

When I work with writers on the plots of scripted comedy, we're always looking to simplify. It's easy to overcomplicate things and it takes a lot of time and crafting to strip out the unnecessary accretions. When we spoke, the first series of *The Cockfields* by Joe Wilkinson and David Earl was about to air. Made by Lucy Lumsden's company Yellow Door Productions, the show is a pitch-perfect marriage of a quirky sensibility with a recognizable relationship dynamic. It's a tale of an everyday relatable situation, boy introduces girlfriend for the first time to eccentric parents, and is closely modelled on the writers' real lives and experiences. Lucy told me:

> David and Joe came together to write about people they knew in a situation that would feel familiar to them. They are rightly obsessed with being authentic and truthful and not leaping on really big comic events that would lose that all important credibility. But as they write, and write and redraft and redraft, there is tendency to funny things up. Some bigger comics set-pieces went in that we all loved and we all got rather attached to. But as they got more confident with the characters and understood them, they realized they didn't need to rely on big, slightly implausible comic constructs in order to deliver the laugh.

It's about detail and truth. Rather than inventing, Joe and David are often saying, 'What would *you* say in this situation? What would you actually do? What *did* you do when your dad said that to you?'

When I'm teaching comedy writing, students often produce extraordinary and outlandish situations for their characters. There is clearly a place for this, but I always encourage writers to try and find the funny in simpler things. Lucy comments:

> I think it's such a good thing for comedy writers to be confident about being simple. You don't need to invent some scenario for it to be funny. The absolute epitome of that is *The Royle Family* – how little happens. You don't need heaps of story. You just need to put your characters together. David and Joe had all their family to draw upon and they also have very truthful experiences that they exaggerated and condensed. They'd compress maybe a week's worth of hell into a day, but they had the security of knowing that these things actually happened. If the situations actually happened, it usually means they haven't been seen before. And if there's one thing you need in comedy, it's surprise. When we worked on *Cockfields*, Joe and David had been working closely with Ricky Gervais. On *After Life*, Ricky's really quite anti-story. He has characters that are very clearly delineated and he just loves to see them hang out together in a scene and see what happens. If the delineations of your character are clear, don't obsess about story. It works very well for Ricky. He's got a very light touch of a story in *After Life*. Very big beats but lightly done and I suspect that influenced David and Joe writing *Cockfields* not to obsess and to think more, 'Let's enjoy this situation and see what comes of it.' And look at Julia Davis. She knows roughly where she's heading but then enjoys the randomness. It is comedy after all. It's not a box-set drama where you'll be patted on the back for the plotting.

From the point of view of improvising a story, Caitlin Campbell told me:

> We actually quite innately have an understanding of story within us. When we teach our beginner storytelling classes, we focus on that: the fact that most of us have a really strong storytelling instinct. When you're an audience member, you actually know what you want to see. Once you're improvising, with all the stress and the fear of having people watching you and having to make all the decisions, those instincts go away because you're scared. Almost everything with improv is just about stress-testing yourself over and over again, until you can relax enough to have your instincts come back and follow them. If you are able to relax enough to make a simple, obvious choice, then narratives can be really easy. They become really hard when everyone is making lots of panicked

choices. But the gift of improv is that shows like that could still be lots of fun! The audience likes watching you try and make sense of it and keep it going. But the really magic shows are the ones where people don't look like they're trying, because the decisions feel like they are making themselves.

Rebecca MacMillan has a fascinating take on how audiences can make stories from the slightest things you give them: 'I think that urge to create story is such a strong inherent human quality that you can push it too hard, you almost don't have to really try. You can be really light touch with it and still create something that satisfies, that ticks the box [so] that people feel like something happened that felt like it could be called a story. Even when we intentionally try not to create a story [in a show], people will see a story!' For example, my daughter Kaia and her friend recently were watching leaves swirl around a deep puddle and the leaves became boats and when they got snagged the boats had stopped because people were getting off and on. A whole narrative emerged from leaves bobbing about in a pool of rainwater.

Be led by your characters

If you try too hard to think of hilarious things for your characters to do, the danger is it will become contrived. In his book *The Comic Hero's Journey*, Steve Kaplan advises writers that 'While you, the author, have God-like powers and can make anything happen in your story, you want to avoid top-down-writing where plot considerations and invention take precedence over character.'[1] Whether you're figuring out your plot in advance, or discovering it as you go, the goal is for your characters to drive the action.

   I see a lot of early drafts of scripts and a common shortcoming is that *stuff just happens to the characters*. As a rule, it's so much stronger when the comedy comes from characters making bad decisions, or making bold decisions that will lead to fallout they are ill equipped to deal with. For example, in the pilot of *Friends* Rachel walks out on her wedding. She isn't left at the altar by the groom. One of Merman's early hit sitcoms was David Cross's *The Increasingly Poor Decisions of Todd Margaret*. Clelia Mountford told me, 'With Todd Margaret, he lies about everything. It's a flaw in his own character that leads him into various predicaments. Terrible things happen because of the wrong decisions he's made.' It's great when characters are the author of their own misfortune in this way – far funnier than being the victim of random bad luck. If a problem really is visited upon your blameless character, then they need to respond to it unskilfully,

---

[1] S. Kaplan, *The Comic Hero's Journey: Serious Story Structure for Fabulously Funny Films*, Studio City, CA: Michael Wiese Productions, 2018, p. 73.

inappropriately or incompetently. This is the 'Basil Fawlty dealing with the body of the dead guest' approach, where in 'The Kipper and the Corpse' episode of *Fawlty Towers* he turns tragedy to farce.

Will Hines, who is starting to write sitcom scripts from his improv background, said, 'The shorthand that I'm currently using is solving problems badly. A problem comes up, you solve it badly, that creates a new problem and you solve that badly and so on.' Basically, have your characters attempt to solve problems in such a way that new problems are created. Will and I discussed how in the 'The Kipper and the Corpse' there is clearly a sensitive and skilful way of dealing with the death of the guest, but the comedy comes from Basil, and his reluctant accomplices Polly and Manuel, ineptly trying to solve the problem. Will remarks:

> If a hotel manager finds a corpse in the room, and it's [short form] improv, so this is the only scene you're going to have, what he does with the corpse is irrelevant. You just want to see his emotional reaction to it and have him focus on all the wrong things, but we'll never move forward. That's something I have to teach a lot in classes. Don't worry about solving it. Within the scope of an improv scene, if you get too focused on solving a problem, you're creating a narrative that we're never going to see. I call it problem-prov. It's the fun you have in being confronted with it. The main difference for me is in improv, problems are irrelevant, and in my sitcom writing, problems are the whole thing. An improv scene that starts with two people trying to pick a lock, they don't ever need to pick the lock for the improv scene. They can make zero progress on that. It doesn't matter what the consequences would be if they did get in because the scene's only going to be three minutes. In a sitcom, two guys picking a lock, well, that's going to lead to the next scene. I need to know the consequences of that problem. There's the game of the scene, which will hopefully be fun, but then I also need by the end of it to have evolved something.

Steve Kaplan posed a question to me:

> Why do characters want to solve their problems? Why do they want to find love, or get out of their dead-end job, or kill their rival, or invent a time machine? It's because human beings want to feel good. There are only two kinds of people in the world who want to feel miserable: poets and actors. Everybody else wants to feel good. If I see the world as a scary place, that makes me nervous, but I can do something about it. I can go home, I can lock my doors, I can turn on music, I can have a drink, I can smoke a cigarette. I can have a pint of Häagen-Dazs ice cream. I can go into my panic room and turn on Bach and I can smile. The whole point is that everybody wants to feel good. Your characters have to go through more of a difficult obstacle course to get there,

but it's the only way they can do it. Even shy people have babies. They must figure out a way to do it. They get around all the obstacles.

Why does Basil want to attract a better class of guest to Fawlty Towers? Why does Fleabag hit on people? Why is Larry David so blunt? They all want to feel good.

In taking action to try and feel good, Steve says comedy characters are trying to win. What would winning look like for your character? They never will win the big prize (of it they do, it's game over), but you can grant them some small victories. Basil will get the occasional satisfaction of getting one over on his wife, or he'll enjoy the simpler pleasure of being rude to a guest, but he never will turn Fawlty Towers into the classy establishment he dreams of it being and to be free of the 'riff raff'. You can apply this thinking to stand-up too. Working with a stand-up recently who I felt was just telling stuff to the audience for no particular reason other than to make them laugh, referencing Steve's work I asked him, 'What's winning for you?' He responded, 'Well, if the audience also agree that my partner's wrong and I'm right, for me, that's winning.' The comedy then came from the fact that if anything the audience were siding with his partner. Going on stage with the intention of winning, you're not just trying to make them laugh, you go on stage to try and validate your point of view and get them to agree with you.

I told Steve this notion of 'winning' had helped the comic, giving him a different and more relatable motivation, and he responded, 'Oh, that's great. Yes, winning works in stand-up. What positive action does is it draws the portrait of your character. It allows us to see who you really are. It shows the stuff that normally in real life we try to hide. Again, in stand-up, the good comic is not just insulting somebody else or criticizing something else: they're exposing themselves.' So when you're developing your stand-up, ask yourself what is it you're trying to achieve? What's winning for *you*?

In order to win, in Steve's model, characters must take *positive action* and in so doing they will also reveal a little of who they are. Steve explained: 'Positive action says that, "I'm going to try to win, I'm going to try to get something and how I'm going to do it is going to reveal who I am".' In attempting to get what he wants in order to feel good with his limited skill set and many deficiencies, Basil Fawlty reveals himself as rude, snobbish and angry. He doesn't set out with the intention of being rude, snobbish and angry! It's a by-product. So, don't, for example, have your characters behave rudely for the sake of being rude. In Steve's terms, they have to be taking positive action to try to win to feel good and that manifests as rudeness! As Steve puts it, 'A positive action exposes me for who I really am.' You might be wondering, how can something negative like being rude be a *positive* action? It needn't be positive to those on the receiving end, it just needs to be the only move the character can take at that point to try to achieve their goal, to win. A more sane, skilful or pragmatic character might choose charm or diplomacy. But all your character has available to them, at that point, is rudeness. John Cleese and Connie Booth show all of Basil's negative traits through him taking positive action. All the fiascos with the corpse in 'The Kipper and the Corpse' come about because he's taking positive action to try to win: to get the body off the premises without any awkwardness or being implicated in any way in the death, and so ultimately to feel good.

If, as a writer or improviser, you think 'In the next scene my character will be sarcastic' without a goal in mind, then this is negative action. Steve Kaplan described a purely negative action to me as 'simply something that doesn't move you any closer to getting what you want'. Maybe your character is being sarcastic about her unfit husband's crazy plan to run a marathon. The sarcasm might be comic, but what is she trying to achieve? What's winning for her? So instead of unmotivated sarcasm, in this example you might think 'My character will try to get her husband to drop his crazy plan to run a marathon having not exercised for twenty years (so she won't have to deal with the fallout) by pointing out the plan's failings in a sarcastic way.' This way, characters are leading the action by attempting to get what they want, to win, to feel good. Therefore, in long-form improv or script writing, when you're trying to work out 'what your character should do next, don't ask: what would be funny? Ask instead: what do they do next to try to win?' In order to win, your character will, in Steve's terms, be taking positive action. Their choices and actions should be guided by a desire to get the outcome they want to feel good, the comedy coming from having to work with the limited tools at their disposal.

Okay, so you've found your engaging characters, you're keeping it simple, it's based in truth and they're all taking positive action to try to win. Now you need some shape and structure to contain all this. And that's where we turn in the final chapter.

Chapter 10
Story Structure

Whether it's entirely whimsical or based on a true story, whether meticulously plotted in advance or made up as you go along, your narrative will feature a manageable number of well drawn, distinct characters with clear goals. It will have a well structured main storyline, and where there are secondary stories there will be a well defined hierarchy of significance, and they will ideally weave together, or reference each other, or at least be strongly linked thematically. But before you tell your story (in whatever form or medium), it really helps if you have a clear premise. Here's a way to test the clarity of your idea. Can you describe your comic premise in seven words? You have seven words (no more, no less) to describe your premise, newspaper-headline style. You are not describing the whole story, just the central idea. For example, here is how I describe the premise of some of the comedy pieces and shows we have discussed at various points in this book (see if you can figure out what they all are!). I'll start off with a couple of easy ones:

'Old man goes down hill in bath'
'Customer returns dead parrot to pet shop'
'Fish dance ends with big fish slap'
'Man's name is sound of dropped lighter'
'Hollywood determines female actor's last fuckable day'

You can do the same thing with a sitcom scene:

'Jelly fish sting leads to urination embarrassment'
'Awkwardness of someone buying you unsolicited dessert'

And for stand-up act-outs:

'Heart attack behaves like a brutal cop'

And with the premise of a sitcom:

'Angry man runs Torquay hotel really badly'

And even a movie:

'Man lives single day over and over'.

Stories and narrative arcs

A clear premise is the springboard to writing anything from a sketch to a sitcom to a film, and part of the challenge of improv is discovering what that premise is while the show is in motion. When it comes to the unfolding of the story in long-form improvisation, Caitlin Campbell of Bristol Improv Theatre told me, 'We use the story design Pixar use in most of the improv groups that I work in. Parallelogramophonograph [or PGraph, from Austin, Texas] taught it to us:

– *once upon a time,*
– *and every single day until one day*
– *and because of that,*
– *and because of that,*
– *and because of that,*
– *until finally . . .'*

Caitlin explains, 'That's the trajectory that your story needs to follow.' She broke it down as follows (and this applies equally to stories you're writing as well as ones you are making up as you go along): 'You need to know: what the world is, where we are, what matters, who we're going to follow within it, and then what changes that takes them on the journey, whether that's a literal journey or an emotional journey, and what has changed by the end? Has the protagonist changed or has the world changed or is it both?' This echoes movie plotting and is the kind of story structure Steve Kaplan writes about in his book *The Comic Hero's Journey*. There is an established reality, which is then disrupted, sending your character on a journey to reach a new equilibrium by the end. Films do tend to have more of a radical change between where the characters start and where they end.

In contrast, sitcom episodes traditionally end with the characters in the same place that they began, not having moved on at all. In this approach, we join our sitcom characters in an already dysfunctional situation, then a problem or challenge is introduced into this world, they go about trying to deal with the issue, they either win or lose, and next episode they're back to square one. Very little, if anything, carries over from one episode to the next and with these kinds of shows you can watch the episodes of any individual series in pretty much any order.

More commonly nowadays, however, you will have self-contained stories in individual episodes *and* a narrative arc that unfolds across a series, ultimately perhaps even over many seasons spanning several years. Top sitcom script consultant and author Marc Blake comments, 'With the predominance of streaming, the sitcom form is now adopting soap or drama-like arcs.' Broadly, there are now three main approaches to TV narrative comedy series:

- Self-contained episodes (the traditional approach);
- Self-contained episodes *and* a series-spanning narrative arc (see below for more on this);
- The series is in serial form; like a movie broken up into episodes.

Fawlty Towers takes the first approach as do some contemporary shows like *The IT Crowd*. An example of the second approach is seen in season 3 of *Curb Your Enthusiasm*. Picking up a theme from Chapter 6, the narrative arc across the series sees Larry David investing in a swanky new restaurant. There are complete, unrelated stories in every episode about, amongst other things, a warning of a terrorist attack, Larry becoming obsessed with a dead man's shirt, and missing his own mother's funeral. The bigger story of the restaurant opening weaves in and out of these episodes, unfolding across the season to its profanity-filled opening night. Some episodes don't even mention the restaurant, but those that do introduce complications along the way, like losing chefs (including the bald one that Larry hired out of follicly motivated solidarity), accidentally breaking a food critic's thumbs and, at the eleventh hour, hiring a French chef with Tourette's (hence the profanity). With this approach, you might hit upon a climactic event to your series and then work out a sequence of steps to get your characters there (with obstacles and reversals along the way). You then distribute these stages of the bigger narrative arc amongst the otherwise self-contained episode stories. *Peep Show* is another show that takes this sort of approach.

Then there is the third, more challenging approach, where your series becomes more like a film in episodic instalments – for example, Daisy Haggard's brilliant *Back to Life*, Vic Reeves and Bob Mortimer's *Catterick* and the second series of *Fleabag*. One challenge of this approach is to break the narrative down into episodes that feel satisfyingly complete in themselves. Another challenge is to have change and development but not too much! You're aiming for a balance of movement and stasis as it's hard to fundamentally change the opening premise, in the way a movie can, and maintain the identity of the show.

For instance, the first series of *Fleabag* is complete in itself, with the overarching story of Fleabag's friend's suicide unfolding across the six episodes. Fleabag's signature relationship with the audience, as she looks into the camera and speaks directly to us, also reaches a conclusion. At the outset it's 'Come in, this is going to be a riot', then at the end of the series it's 'Go away from me, stop looking at me.' This relationship with the audience, born out of the original stage monologue, existed because Fleabag had something to confess to us. Once the confession has been made, and we the audience know her secret, why would that relationship with the camera continue? In order to bring the series back, Phoebe Waller-Bridge had to devise a new premise, the pursuit of Andrew Scott's 'Hot Priest', as he became known, while keeping key elements of the original series in place, including this crucial direct address to the camera. But why is she still talking with us? She decided it's simply that we are now hanging around and she can't get rid of us. This underlines how modern sitcoms/comedy dramas can change over time, but not too much. A Fleabag who doesn't talk to the camera would cease to be Fleabag.

Developing stories

Having looked at the bigger picture, let's now explore the nitty-gritty of story structure. While well-meaning but non-specialist reviewers of long-form improvisation shows often write comments like 'I really couldn't tell which bits were improvised and which bits were planned', in truth, with improv, you don't have the luxury of preparing scenes in advance, let alone plotting out the whole story. Inevitably you start at scene 1 and then work your way to the end, discovering everything as you go. The skill of it is to embrace this rather than attempting, within the improvisation, to plot ahead. As Katy Schutte explained to me, 'If you've decided what the rest of the story is at any point, you're fucked, because however many people are on stage, if they've all done that, you might have six to ten different stories. Then everyone is fighting for what should happen and telling other people what to do. Whereas, if you just go moment to moment then we're good. But if you say something like "In three hours there'll be a meeting in the library", now we have to remember to do that scene. That's hard work. You have to remember things and you have to do it in the right order.'

Katy told me how Baby Wants Candy, the improvised musical team, say 'Do it now'. Meaning that if they get a suggestion from the audience that the show is called 'The Prom' for example, rather than building up to the prom as the finale, as you may well do across a TV series or in a movie, they'll take that as their starting-point. Katy said:

Our feeling as writers is, 'Great, I'll make all the characters build up to the prom. It will be big the event.' But as an improviser, they say do the prom in scene 1, and then the rest of the show is the fallout of the prom. Then you don't have to all try and align to this one spot. I guess it's like if you've jumped out of a plane and you're trying to hit this one tiny field with your parachute, it may or may not work, and then the audience will feel disappointed that you haven't landed the thing. You haven't gone in the right field. If no one's decided what field it is, then we're like, 'Great. You landed. Good job. That was fun.' I think not getting ahead of ourselves and making future promises in improv is important.

However, when *writing* a narrative comedy script I wouldn't recommend starting at scene 1 and writing to the end with absolutely no sense of where it's going! But if you *are* someone who likes to write your way into an idea, you might take a leaf out of the Coen brothers' book. While they will have a strong sense of time, place, themes and maybe some incidents and structural thoughts, as Ethan says they don't write an outline of the plot, and don't generally know what's going to happen later in the story, when they're still writing the early stages.[1] That way your characters are free to act as they wish, and scene by scene you will discover the story. Or you might alternatively take the *set-pieces* approach. This is where you write a whole load of entirely disconnected scenes, in effect sketches, featuring your characters and then select scenes to be part of a longer narrative. (A solo stand-up show can also be built around set-pieces. In this case, your set-pieces are the stand-out stories, gags and routines that the show is built around. See my first book, *A Director's Guide to the Art of Stand-up*, for more on this.)

One of your stand-alone scenes might feel like the call to action of an episode. This is the event that sets the story of that episode in motion. Or you might have hit upon a particularly outlandish scene that feels like an end to an episode. Then you can figure out how to get your characters there. Or you might have a scene that has a 'middle of an episode' feel. For example, in the 'Are You Right There, Father Ted?' episode of the wonderful *Father Ted*, there's a scene where Ted is looking out of the window and gesticulating angrily, and a square patch of dirt happens to line up with his top lip, making him look to people outside alarmingly reminiscent of Hitler. This began life as a single set-piece idea without any context. From that starting-point, writers Graham Linehan and Arthur Matthews then wrote the scenes that happened before and after.

The episode begins with a teaser where Ted has been promoted and is in a luxurious parish in Dublin enjoying the good life, but a financial irregularity with church expenses means Ted is deported back to the godforsaken Craggy Island (the church's dumping ground for troublesome priests). In sitcom, you often find a *teaser* and a *kicker* bookending the episode (otherwise known as the 'cold open' and the 'tag'). These are mini sketches featuring your characters that top and tail the show, which may or not be strongly linked with the plot. The 'teaser' and 'kicker' are American devices (originally due to US commercial breaks, but

---

[1] D. Jenkins, 'The Coen brothers: It Goes Where It Goes', *Little White Lies*, n.d., https://lwlies.com/interviews/the-coen-brothers-inside-llweyn-davis/.

now often found in UK sitcom too). The teaser slot, by the way, can be a good place to drop in short, funny scenes you've written that don't neatly slot into a narrative. They are also an excellent way of showcasing your comedy writing chops on page 1 of a script you're pitching.

In this *Father Ted* episode, the narrative proper begins with Ted discovering a fellow priest, alarmingly, has a huge amount of Nazi regalia, which is sowing the seeds of a problem later on when Ted will unwittingly inherit it all following the priest's untimely death. This is followed by Ted and Dougal needing to do the cleaning due to housekeeper Mrs Doyle falling off the roof and injuring her back. Then we get the call to action of the episode. In order to entertain Dougal while they do the cleaning, Ted puts a lampshade on his head like an Asian conical hat and playfully acts out a pantomime stereotype of a Chinese man.

Unfortunately, three Chinese people are outside the window watching him. Ted is aghast; he is fully aware he has been caught acting out a racist stereotype. He is also puzzled as to what the Chinese people are doing on this remote, sparsely populated island off the west coast of Ireland. Dougal explains to him that Craggy Island has a big Chinese community, which is news to Ted. From this lampshade incident, rumours spread across the island that Ted is racist. His attempts to clear his name are undermined by the unfortunate Hitler-moustache– window incident which was the seed of the whole episode. From there, he attempts to refute the idea that he is racist by staging a diversity event. Just when he seems to have cleared his name, his good work is undone when Chinese community leaders visit him and see the huge amount of inherited Nazi regalia that poor Ted was unaware had been delivered. Since *Father Ted* follows a traditional sitcom form of self-contained stories, none of this follows on to subsequent episodes and the sudden introduction of a large Chinese community on this remote island, which has never featured before and is never referred to again, is doable due to the cartoon nature of the show.

How *you* approach constructing a narrative is down to your own creative inclinations. You might be drawn to writing set-piece scenes as a starting-point, like *Father Ted* writers Graham Linehan and Arthur Matthews; or maybe, like Larry David on *Curb Your Enthusiasm*, you're more of a plot-first writer. As we discussed in Chapter 1, the plots of *Curb Your Enthusiasm* are meticulously crafted, but the actors improvise the dialogue. David will lovingly collect examples of bad behaviour, faux pas and social embarrassment and from this store of raw ingredients will cook up the plotlines of *Curb*. The skill of it is in bringing together storylines from the great mass of possibilities and having them dovetail elegantly.

Another show where the plot is worked out first, but this time with scripted dialogue, is *Peep Show*. When they began work on each series, writers Sam Bain and Jessie Armstrong would spend six weeks coming up with every idea they could: funny ideas, set-pieces, narrative arcs for characters to travel on, and characters to come into the show. They wouldn't suppress or censor anything at this stage. Later, they'd start narrowing it down to which ideas would go into each episode. Then they'd spend about two weeks per episode plotting out what will happen exactly, scene by scene. Once all six episodes of the series had been plotted in this way, they'd then begin writing the scenes and the dialogue, which after all the hard work of developing the plots would feel like the fun bit.[2]

Fawlty Towers also began with plotting. When they were developing the stories for this intricately plotted farce, John Cleese and Connie Booth would plot out the storylines in flowcharts on the reverse of an unfurled roll of wallpaper. They'd be constantly refining it until it was running like clockwork. Only when an entire episode had been plotted did they write any dialogue. The starting-points for the stand-alone stories and situations in *Fawlty Towers* tended to be real-life problems from the hotel industry that their characters would set about making a total hash of dealing with: from big problems like a guest dying to more everyday problems like supplying food and drink when ingredients or staff are not available (or indeed when the chef is drunk and incapable as in the 'Gourmet Night' episode). Their own experiences were supplemented by conversations with people in the hotel and hospitality industry. For example, a former employee of the Savoy Hotel named Andrew Leeman told them his biggest challenge was having to deal with 'the stiffs' – the (typically elderly) guests who had died while staying at the hotel – and getting the body out without upsetting the other guests. And so 'The Kipper and the Corpse' episode was born and the deceased guest was named Mr Leeman in Andrew's honour.

Acts, plotlines and dramatic irony

When you're putting a story together, it really helps to think in terms of the three-act structure. Typically acts 1 and 3 are shorter, with act 2 being the meat of it. My SREP model of scene structure, which I discuss in Chapter 5, maps onto these three acts:

Act 1: The set-up/reveal of the episode: the challenges for your characters are set in motion.

Act 2: The escalation: a series of complications arise and things get worse and more challenging.

Act 3: The payoff: the climactic scenes where things come to a head or are resolved with a twist at the end.

---

[2] A. Musson, 'Mustard Interview: Sam Bain & Jesse Armstrong', *Mustard*, n.d., http://www.mustardweb.org/peepshow/.

The story structure Caitlin Campbell describes above can also be looked at in terms of the classic three-act structure:

Act 1: Once upon a time, and every single day until one day . . .

Act 2: . . .and because of that, and because of that, and because of that . . .

Act 3: . . . until finally.

You can write stories in four, five or even seven acts, but three works well for comedy and is a natural structure as it's basically beginning, middle and end (with a teaser and a kicker bookending it). You might have one strong plotline that affects all the characters, like the *Father Ted* episode described above. Or alternatively – and this is a common approach in TV narattive comedy – your story will have a number of plotlines that unfold more or less independently and then collide at the end: the A plot being the main story and then various subplots: the B plot, C plot and so on. Here, for example, are the plotlines of the very first episode of *Friends*, which we discussed in the previous chapter:

A PLOT – Rachel walking out on her wedding and walking in on old friend Monica. Losing her financial support from her father. Moving in with the friends. Getting a job as a waitress. Taking an interest in Ross.

B PLOT – Ross dealing with his girlfriend coming out as a lesbian, moving out and taking a lot of the furniture with her. Taking an interest in Rachel.

C PLOT – Monica dating Paul the wine guy. Falling for his line. Finding out it is a line. Then rejecting him.

A, B and C plots can be found in improv too. Caitlin Campbell gave an example: 'The improvised *Sherlock* shows will tend to have three storylines. One of them is Holmes and Watson, one of them is the person whose case is being investigated, and the third is either the villain's or people who are affected by the situation.' In long-form improv, in common with scripted plotting, as improviser Rebecca MacMillan told me, 'You're looking for all the various threads to wrap up in a way that feels natural.' Sometimes, however, the fact that it can be rather contrived can be part of the enjoyment: '*Sherlock* for instance almost makes a joke of things being all crowbarred together in the last scene. It's like, "Wow, we've got lots to tie up here, but we're going to make that fast, cool and funny and the audience is going to love it when we've remembered something from the first scene and we bring it back and that ties everything up, even if it feels a little bit crowbarred."' Caitlin adds, 'Sometimes, you go into the final scene of *Sherlock* with absolutely no idea how you're going to solve it. Other times you have the perfect solution where you're thinking, "This is amazing. It's going to knock them dead."' But as Caitlin ruefully points out, you might have overlooked something that contradicts your solution and then you're left desperately trying to fix the plot hole. She said you might triumphantly name the murderer only for someone else to point out that the supposed murderer was actually in the room with you at the time of the murder. Then, she said, 'you're scrabbling for a solution like, "No, it was his identical twin."' Those moments, that can be hilarious in improv, would be deeply frustrating for the audience in scripted comedy. Plot issues do come up in the development of scripted comedy all the time, of course, but there you have time and space to mull over various options and you can go back and change earlier scenes to fix the kind of problem Caitlin describes.

Looking to practise what I preach, this book also has an A, B and C plot! The A plot is about creating comedy narratives, the B plot is how techniques and approaches cross different forms of comedy and there's a little, personal, C plot thread running through concerning my daughter Kaia and my partner Kate! As with classic comedy narrative structure, all three plotlines collide at the end: in the last paragraph of this chapter. The C plot narrative, by the way, begins with a teaser in the form of the dedication at the front of the book and then, if you look carefully, concludes with a kicker in the footnotes. Returning to TV comedy, in 'The Kipper and the Corpse' episode of *Fawlty Towers*, the A plot is dealing with the deceased guest, the B plot is elderly Mrs Chase wanting her dog to be pampered (much to Basil's disdain) and the C plot is simply the doctor, who happens to be staying, *really* wanting some sausages. The only reason the doctor is on the premises, by the way, is that the plot requires one. They don't, however, just have him hanging around waiting for the demise of a guest. He has to have a goal of his own, hence wanting sausages. And since there's no story without obstacles to a character's desire, it's a real struggle for him to get them. Which reminds me that a few years ago at Bath Spa University, one of the sitcom students had created a great fool in a show set in a student union bar, but he wasn't really doing anything apart from hanging around saying stupid things. He needed a goal. Thinking of the doctor, I suggested that he wants chips. But what's stopping him from getting them? The simple answer was he has no money. Watching the fool trying to get chips, despite being the C plot, became a highlight of the show. Importantly he tried lots of different ways to get them, from flattery to theft to blackmail. Whether it's improvised or written, mix up the approaches your characters take to achieve their goals. And whether the desire is as big as avoiding any problems associated with a dead body or as small as getting chips (or sausages), if your character *really* wants it, it will help drive the action forward and make it more compelling to watch.

As a farce, there is *a lot* of dramatic irony in 'The Kipper and the Corpse', including a scene that takes a classic bedroom farce situation and gives it a macabre spin. When I spoke with improviser Caitlin Campbell, we discussed dramatic irony and, as an example, I described this kind of scene where you'd have the wife in her bedroom with the lover who has come round for some morning love-making now her husband has gone to work. Just as things are hotting up, they hear the husband unexpectedly coming back into the house, so her lover quickly hides in the wardrobe. As the wife tries to calm down and appear nonchalant, the husband comes into the bedroom and we discover he has returned home to get his tie which he needs to wear in an important meeting that day. But when he goes to get his tie out of the wardrobe, his wife stops him saying, 'Ties, they're so formal. They're so stuffy and out of date. Don't wear a tie to your meeting, you'll look more relaxed.' He'll reply, 'I just want my tie, what's your problem?' The whole engine of the scene is that the audience know the lover is in the wardrobe but the husband doesn't: dramatic irony. I asked Caitlin about dramatic irony in improv and she responded, 'It happens all the time. What you've described could easily happen as an improv scene because as an improviser, it's about fostering the thing that's going to be really juicy to the audience. There's so much opportunity in that. If I was playing a husband and as I walk into a scene the lover has gone into a wardrobe, I would really have missed a trick if I didn't find reasons to want to look in the wardrobe. That tension and release is something that you really recognize in improv a lot.'

In a nod to this kind of classic bedroom farce scene, in 'The Kipper and the Corpse', Basil – along with a reluctant Manuel and Polly – have carried Mr Leeman's body out of his room whereupon resident guest Miss Tibbs sees the deceased and becomes hysterical. On Basil's urging, Polly slaps her to bring her to her senses – but she applies too much force and knocks her out cold. In a panic, they manhandle both the unconscious Miss Tibbs and the corpse into a nearby empty bedroom and hide them in the wardrobe. At which point – like the unfaithful wife's husband – the couple who are staying in the room – a Mr and Mrs White – return and, of course, want to get something from their wardrobe. Having an unconscious pensioner and a dead body inside is certainly upping the ante on the classic 'hidden lover' scenario!

The highpoint of dramatic irony in the episode is when Mr Leeman's colleagues come back 'to collect him', Basil mistakenly assumes they are undertakers but we the audience know full well who they are. By this point Leeman's body has been dumped in the laundry basket with the used sheets and towels. His colleagues are naturally bemused when upon asking Basil where Mr Leeman is, they are met with the conspiratorial response: 'He's in the basket.' Earlier in the episode, Sybil was shown sorting out the laundry for the laundrymen to sow the seeds for this moment. A big part of making a story unfold satisfyingly for an audience, whether it's a complex farce like *Fawlty Towers*, an absurdist cartoon like *Father Ted* or a slower and less incident-packed single camera comedy drama like *Detectorists*, is sowing seeds for later incidents. As you work out your story you might make discoveries that involve doubling back and rewriting earlier scenes in order to foreshadow (or at least not contradict) your new discoveries.

At the climax of 'The Kipper and the Corpse episode, all the plotlines collide in classic style. In the A plot, finally Mr Leeman's colleagues are informed of his death by Sybil (as usual, the professional one), while for complicated reasons Basil has hidden the body behind the hat stand in the lobby, disguising it with a hat. (Again, dramatic irony as *we* know why Basil is stood awkwardly against the hat stand but Mr Leeman's shocked and baffled departing colleagues don't.) Then there's a commotion as all the guests who have been wronged in the episode converge on the front desk to complain to Sybil: Miss Tibbs (still in shock) and Mr and Mrs White (whose wardrobe was requisitioned) along with – *B plot* – Mrs Chase (whose dog is ill from Tabasco sauce a disgruntled Polly had put on its food) and – *C plot* – Dr Price, who finally resorted to cooking his own sausages but then discovered they were out of date – a false dawn ending to his plotline. In a final moment of dramatic irony, we see Basil making his getaway by hiding himself in the laundry basket which the laundrymen take away. Sybil, however, has no idea where he's gone as she once again has to sort out the chaos Basil has caused. Like *Father Ted*, none of this will have any bearing on future episodes. Where an entire series does have an overarching narrative, it can be useful to break down the stories that span the entire season in the same way as you would a single episode. For example, the narratives unfolding across the second series of *Fleabag* are:

A STORY: Fleabag and the Priest;

B STORY: Fleabag's sister Clare's marriage troubles;

C STORY: Her godmother and father's wedding.

These reference each other and overlap of course, but they are broadly three independent stories. And then there's the crucial D story of Fleabag's relationship with the viewing audience that itself develops and unfolds across the series. (I've broken it down into A, B, C and D reflecting the amount of screen time each story commands, from most to least.) If you're working in this way, while I'm sure there's software that can do this for you, I always feel you can't beat the old-fashioned tactile approach with, for example, each story broken down into beats across multiple colour coded post-it notes that you can have on the wall and shift about into a sequence of episodes. Phoebe Waller-Bridge herself described her writing process as taking place in bed with post-its (she says she can't write in cafes) and at times in an office with her producers, where they'll put all her notes on the wall, talk about them for hours and move them around into various configurations.[3] And when we spoke about Aisling Bea's series *This Way Up* (see Chapter 1), producer Clelia Mountford told me, 'When it comes to

[3] Lucy Prebble, 'Phoebe Waller-Bridge: "There was an alternative ending to Fleabag . . . but I'll never tell"', *Guardian*, 9 November 2019, https://www.theguardian.com/books/2019/nov/09/phoebe-waller-bridge-alternative-ending-fleabag.

making a second series, she'll come here to the London office. We've got a writers' room with whiteboards on the wall. She can come in and sit with us and we can help shape it because again, she's got great ideas for a second series but there's so much!'

The heart of the narrative

To bring things full circle, let's return to the subject of true stories with which we began the book. As we've seen, even your fictions will be informed by your own experiences and your research, but sometimes a show is openly autobiographical. The Hopwood Depree stand-up show that I directed, *The Manc is a Yank*, which I discuss in Chapter 1, unfolded in this way: 'Once upon a time there was an actor living that Hollywood lifestyle in LA . . . and he did that *every single day* . . . *until one day* while researching his ancestry online he discovered he was heir to a crumbling stately home in the north of England *and because of that* he moved to England to try to save the hall . . . *and because of that* he developed an odd-couple relationship with hall caretaker Bob . . . *and because of that* he ended up having to do a range of specialized and practical jobs he was ill-equipped for . . . *and finally* . . . Well, 'and finally' is a problem in this case because he's still in the thick of it all. The true story doesn't yet have an ending.

When working with a true story, you often face challenging questions. Where do you start and end it? Whose story is it? What themes are you concentrating on? Even non-fiction writers have to make these editing and selecting decisions. You have to carve a beginning, middle and end out of open-ended reality. Hopwood reflected, 'When we initially started to develop the show, we had a lot of material about me finding out about the house, about the decision to move to the UK, interactions with friends and family and agents and managers – and all that was laid out in the first act of the show. I think what we quickly determined was that people just want to jump right into it. It was an important step in the development of the show. It needed to go through that stage but ultimately, we didn't use it.' Act 2, where he was now in the north of England grappling with the hall, became act 1. Instead of the previous 12 minutes of material on the backstory, we put a video at the front of the show to bring people up to speed. Hopwood explains, 'Because my background is in film making, and because the story had a bit of a Hollywood element to it, the decision was made to do a two-minute video that very quickly told the backstory in a humorous way to launch the show, where everybody is immediately up to speed even if you knew nothing about the story walking into it.'

To create the narrative, from the complex real situation, we firstly carved out our bosses, striver, fool and foil. Hopwood is the *striver*, Bob the caretaker is the *boss* and Hopwood's (fictionalized) American agents Shelia and Ken, who don't understand or sympathize with the project, are the *fools*. Meanwhile, the good people of Rochdale and Manchester are the *foils*! In terms of the narrative, Hopwood recalled, 'The A storyline was my journey: the actual physical journey and the emotional journey. Then my ancestry and the characters from the past are a B storyline. This was about finding these various characters from 100 years ago, 200 years ago, 300 years ago and trying to give them life and give them a voice and having those stories run in parallel with mine.' Striking the right balance with the historical information was a challenge: 'We knew it had to have a lot of history because it's dating back over centuries. Finding that balance of the right amount of history with the right amount of humour was tricky in a show like this.' Regarding the B plot strand, at times it was overtaking the A plot. There was a lot of fascinating historical facts but in an early preview we got feedback that at times it became too much like a lecture, albeit an entertaining one. It occurred to me then that rather than Hopwood saying historical facts to the audience, they could come through a character. I said, 'We could really do with a character who can say the historical stuff', thinking we'd make one up. But Hopwood responded, 'There *is* one. The local historian Geoff.' That was a really rewarding moment to realize that the show needed a particular character and to discover that person existed in real life!

The C plot involved our version of Hopwood's agent and her uncomprehending reaction to his choices. Trying to find an endpoint that felt satisfying was difficult, given that the real-life story is very much ongoing and the hall restoration is a project that will take many years. Hopwood admits, 'It was a challenge. And so the conclusion we came to is that [the ending] needed to be about the emotional journey. Me having a better understanding of who I was, why I was on this madcap adventure and better relationships with the other characters, which helped smooth over my fish-out-of-water element.' In the end, because it's a stand-up show, it looks like Hopwood has just come up and started telling the story as casually as he might do to friends in the pub. All of the work is hidden for it to feel like a natural off-the-cuff telling of it. As Hopwood explains, 'Yes even though we have these prepared photos and prepared video, you really also wanted to feel very casual and that people could shout out and say things because it's stand-up. The show is different each night and there will be interaction with the audience and it could change and shift based on what they said or how they were involved in it. I liked that live element of it and that made it fun to perform.' In Hopwood's show, at the end he finds a deeper meaning to the project (A plot) through finding out the history of his ancestors who died in the First World War (B plot), and he faces down his agents who want him to return to Hollywood and turn the whole thing into a cash-in movie (C plot).

Reflecting on the deaths of his more distant ancestors led Hopwood to discuss the more recent deaths of his own father and grandfather. Hopwood recalled, 'It was challenging to decide if and when I should include a poignant moment in the show. Ultimately, since my story was an after effect of my father and grandfather passing away, we felt I had to include this so the audience would have an understanding of the decisions I had made. I was worried that if it became too serious it would be tricky to get the audience back to the comedy. But in the end, it seemed to help. It gave the audience a moment of pause, and for me to connect with them on a deeper level. Moving on to more humorous material then seemed to happen naturally, in the same way it does in real life, since we as humans quite often use humour to ease the heaviness of our own tragedies.' If you can find these moments of pathos in your narrative, it can create more of a connection for the audience with the story and the characters and then the sudden shift back to levity creates a release and, if done abruptly, the comedy of a jarring change of tone. It's like the big laugh at a wake.

Prolific comedy writer and former stand-up Shaun Pye's BBC sitcom *There She Goes* was based on a very personal true story. Producer Clelia Mountford told me, 'He has a profoundly learning-disabled daughter and with *There She Goes*, he finally felt ready to tell the story.'

Shaun's wife contributed substantially to the script to create a rounded view of the situation and there would have been many outside eyes helping develop the project. Clelia notes, 'We all need that distance, which is why it helps writing with a producer or a co-writer or a script editor.' And once again it's about condensing the reality:

> It's not going to be a biographical account of everything that happened. You've still got to craft a story. You've still got your A, B, C plot rather than having a series of disparate conversations or events. But at the same time, you try to be true. With *There She Goes*, Shaun didn't want anything in there that was contrived. Because he's a comedy writer, his natural instinct is to do a callback and dovetail A, B and C . . . He really wanted to resist that, but he would bring stories together under a theme. For example, an episode might be about communication or misunderstanding. Then he could find stories that happened on that theme both in the past and in the present, and by bringing them together we can see the distance she's come. He'd also take events that happened over three months, for example, and condense them into two days. It's makes a better story if you can compact it. It was still stuff that happened. He didn't make anything up. It's getting that distance and perspective and thinking, what is this about? What is this episode going to look at? Rather than just 'oh that happened, and then that happened.' You see the overall arc of the series. It's great to have so much stuff, but then you structure it. You don't have to tell everything.

Clelia adds, 'Only Shaun could have written that story as it was about coping with this particular disabled child and her learning disability and their own particular characters. Those are the best stories because you're not getting someone else to write it who hasn't lived it.' Telling these stories in a comedy context felt risky at first, but with great skill and sensitivity the results were profoundly touching for the audience, especially for people in similar situations. Clelia recalls, 'The response was overwhelming. Shaun was just inundated. It was wonderful. Also, it was good for him and Sarah, his wife, to get that response because they had felt quite isolated. Plus it *is* funny! Some of the things their daughter does are hilarious and it's just good to gain that distance to say, "Actually, this is quite funny." It's like the Chaplin quote, "Life is a tragedy when seen in close-up, but a comedy in long-shot."'

Having considered two narratives based on true stories, let's close with a fiction. In 2019 I directed and was dramaturg of the comedy play *You Only Live Forever*, written by Roxy Dunn and Alys Metcalf. It was seen at Assembly in the Edinburgh Festival Fringe that year and later at Soho Theatre in London. (When I'm a 'dramaturg', incidentally, I do the same work helping shape and develop the material as when I 'script edit'. Just with a fancier title.) The premise of the play was that one of the characters, played by Alys, becomes immortal and eternally youthful, and has the heartbreak of watching her wife, played by Roxy, age and die. The narrative covers hundreds of years, but the key scene comes about sixty years into the story (we join them when they meet in their twenties) with the death of Roxy's character. The original draft of this scene was written in a very playful jokey way, and indeed was very funny. It didn't, however, have any sense of the writers caring about this profound moment in their characters' lives. Looking for that moment of pathos, I said to them, 'Now go back and write the sincere version of that scene where you care about these people and what's happening to them.'

This second version of Roxy's character's death was very touching. We rehearsed this scene entirely straight, looking to play the emotion of the moment. Then when we had taken the audience to the most poignant point, I then had them explode it with a piece of ludicrous physical comedy. With the elderly Roxy's character slumped dead in her armchair, we hear Freddie Mercury singing an emotional passage from 'Who Wants to Live Forever', Alys puts her arms around Roxy and, as the emotion of the moment heightens, she suddenly starts making the corpse dance to the music and when Mercury hits a high note she opens the mouth of the body to mime along. We were a little nervous that such a massive leap from the very touching to the very stupid would be too much, but we needn't have worried. The first time we did a preview (and from then onwards), when Alys started making the cadaver dance, the audience erupted with laughter. It worked because they'd gone somewhere so genuine and so sincere, and were so invested, that when we exploded that moment, it was a huge laugh. We never would have found that really big laugh if the writers hadn't cared about their characters and the situation they were in. In terms of performing that moment, when we spoke for the book Roxy recalled,

All three of us knew it was really important for the sincerity of the death scene to land in order to then get the full comic payoff when Alys' character breaks the moment by making me dance and mime along to the song like a puppet. So I worked with Chris on developing a believable 90-year-old – how do they walk? Speak? Breathe? I remember Chris trying to get my voice to sound more breathless which really unlocked the final moment before she dies, as she essentially runs out of breath. I had to balance the weakness of her voice with also being audible though so I had to cheat a bit and have her louder than she likely would have been in real life. When it came to performing it, I could feel the tension in the room build as the audience often became moved – and then hear the relief in their laughter when Alys broke the moment with the puppetry.

It was a great pleasure one week in the summer of 2019 to take my partner Kate[4] and my daughter Kaia to see *You Only Live Forever* at Soho Theatre. Kaia, then aged ten, had never seen anything I'd directed before and she was really inspired seeing these two brilliant young women in a sell-out show. We stayed a few nights in London and we were also able to take in another of my shows, Hopwood Depree's *The Manc is a Yank*, which was playing that week as part of the Camden Fringe *and* one night we stayed in and listened to the pilot of the Wisebowm sitcom, that I'd helped develop and script edited, on BBC Radio 4! That was quite a week for me. I mention it here partly to blow one's own trumpet, but mainly to make the point that this mix of true and fictional stories, live and broadcast, were all underpinned by the same fundamental techniques and approaches that I have discussed in this book.

---

[4] In the acknowledgements of my first book, I describe Kate Dineen as 'my wife'. At that point we had been engaged for about ten years (!) so I thought that describing her as my wife in print would force us to tie the knot. Somehow we didn't get round to it. We still haven't, even though she is once again described as my wife in the acknowledgements of this book. Maybe we'll finally be married by book three.

Suggested Further Reading

Besser Matt, Ian Roberts and Matt Walsh. *The Upright Citizens Brigade Comedy Improvisation Manual*. New York: Comedy Council of Nicea, LLC, 2013.

Blake, Marc. *How NOT to Write a Sitcom: 100 Mistakes to Avoid If You Ever Want to Get Produced*. London: Bloomsbury, 2011.

Double, Oliver. *Getting the Joke: The Art of Stand-up Comedy*. London: Methuen Drama, 2005.

Head, Chris. *A Director's Guide to the Art of Stand-up*. London: Methuen Drama, 2018.

Hines, Will. *How to Be the Greatest Improviser on Earth*. n.p.p.: Pretty Great Publishing, 2016.

Jagodowski, T. J. and David Pasquesi with Pam Victor. *Improvisation at the Speed of Life: The TJ & Dave Book*. Chicago: Solo Roma, 2015.

Kaplan, Steve. *The Hidden Tools of Comedy: The Serious Business of Being Funny*. Studio City, CA: Michael Wiese Productions, 2013.

Kaplan, Steve. *The Comic Hero's Journey: Serious Story Structure for Fabulously Funny Films*. Studio City, CA: Michael Wiese Productions, 2018.

Lanyon, Andrew. *Bifurcated Thought: Reflections on Inventive Thinking*. Falmouth: Falmouth Art Gallery, 2014.

Schutte, Katy. *The Improviser's Way*. London: Nick Hern Books, 2018.

Thank you for reading. You can take a Writing Narrative Comedy course and a Writing Stand-up Comedy one with me online with the British Comedy Guide. If you want a workshop, a director or a script-editor, you can find more out about me and what I offer at www.chrishead.com. If you want to share any comedy you have developed as a result of reading this book, or if you have a question about comedy, please do drop me a line at chris@chrishead.com.

Index